THE SHYSTER'S DAUGHTER

THE SHYSTER'S DAUGHTER

a memoir

PAULA PRIAMOS

etruscan press

Etruscan Press
Wilkes University
84 West South Street
Wilkes-Barre, PA 18766
(570) 408-4546

WILKES UNIVERSITY

www.etruscanpress.org

Published 2012 by Etruscan Press
Printed in the United States of America
Design by Julianne Popovec
The text of this book is set in Electra LT Std.

First Edition

12 13 14 15 16 5 4 3 2 1

Library of Congress Cataloguing-in-Publication Data

Priamos, Paula.
   The Shyster's Daughter : a memoir / Paula Priamos. – 1st ed.
       p. cm.
   Includes bibliographical references and index.
   ISBN 978-0-9832944-3-6 (alk. paper)
   1. Priamos, Paula. 2. Fathers and daughters–California–Biography.
   3. Greek American women–California–Biography. I. Title.
   HQ755.86.P74 2012
   306.874'2–dc23

Please turn to the back of this book for a list of the sustaining funders of Etruscan Press.

This book is printed on recycled, acid-free paper.

Although this work contains descriptions of people in my life, many of their names and other identifying characteristics have been altered to protect their privacy.

For my father
S'agapo

Shyster (*U.S. slang.*)

1. A lawyer who practices in an unprofessional or tricky manner; especially, one who haunts the prisons and lower courts to prey on petty criminals.

—*Oxford English Dictionary*

Acknowledgments

I would like to express my gratitude to Philip Brady, Robert Lunday, Starr Troup, Julianne Popovec, and Jim Cihlar at Etruscan Press. For their friendship, wit, and humor, I would like to thank Annica Jin-Hendel, Mary Ann Brown, Michelle Seward, Naoko Kato, and Betty Pires. Special thanks goes to my teaching colleague Jackie Rhodes. With much love, I would like to thank my family—my mother, sister, and brother Nick who lived many of these stories with me along with my stepsons. This show of thanks also includes my niece and my sister-in-law Jennifer Priamos. And lastly, with deep appreciation to my husband Jim Brown for his affection and unyielding support at all the right times.

An excerpt of *The Shyster's Daughter* has appeared in ZYZZYVA and in the *Los Angeles Times Magazine* in different form.

THE SHYSTER'S DAUGHTER

PROLOGUE:
A LESSON IN MORAL TURPITUDE

The last time my father calls is shortly before the anniversary of his disbarment to tell me he's just cheated death. On his end, there's background noise—a restaurant, a bar or somewhere far sleazier. Since the divorce he licks his wounds at a topless strip club in Garden Grove called the Kat Nip.

"This *malaka* in a ski mask tried to carjack me. He had a gun to the window and told me to get out of my own goddamn car." My father slows down, hanging on to the moment as if speaking to a jury. "But I gave him the finger and backed the hell out of there."

Considering my father's Greek temper, it doesn't surprise me that he flipped off a gunman before thinking of the possible consequences. Carjacking a middle-aged man for his old diesel Mercedes seems beyond desperate, more like a junkie looking for an easy mark. The days when my father tipped big from a money clip of C-notes in his pocket are gone, along with his law license.

Now he carries ones and fives to slip under the g-strings of his favorite girls at the Kat Nip.

"You're lucky he didn't kill you," I say. If death didn't get him in the form of an actual bullet, it could've gotten him from shock. Priamos men are known for strong minds and weak hearts. My grandfather died at fifty-nine, my father's age. I hear it in his voice. For once, my father sounds scared.

As his daughter, the one child out of three who stuck around, I stay on the line. I listen. It's what I've always done.

"Where were you?" I ask. From my Uncle Dimitri I've learned my father is seeing "a burlesque dancer" known as Sugar Brown. She lives in Compton, the neighboring city of Lynwood where my father grew up.

"In the parking lot at the Bicycle Club."

With the card casino's security cameras and well-lit lots, the evidence is stacked against him. He's lying. After more than two decades spent as a defense attorney heatedly releasing himself and his clients of any wrong doing, my father is cool to the truth. I doubt he'd even know how to recognize it.

"Look," he starts. "That isn't why I called, Paula Girl."

"It isn't?"

"I know you're in love. Things are all good and well. That's great." My father huffs, always the lawyer, leading up to his point. "Just don't let him make you lose sight of what you really want."

He's referring to my fiancé, Jim, whom he recently met at dinner. Right after the salads were served and before Jim came back from the restroom, my father told me he saw the signs, the signs that instead of warning me away, only drew me closer. "Be careful, Paula Girl. I like him, and it doesn't really matter that he's older and already has kids. But his face is bloated. He's an alcoholic. Things trouble him too much. That's probably why his first marriage broke up."

I take the cordless phone into the family room where I check the cuckoo clock, a rather obnoxious engagement gift from my father, suggesting I'm crazy for wanting to marry this guy. We live in Lake Arrowhead, over an hour's drive from the Kat Nip. And that's exactly where he's at because I hear the D.J. announcing "Naughty Natalie," the next girl up on stage with classic Billy Idol belting out, "In the midnight hour, she wants more, more, more . . . "

After another five minutes, I'll come up with an excuse, a late dinner I need to cook or a moonlit walk to the water with my fiancé.

"Jesus, Dad," I say. "So what if I love him. It's not like I've had a lobotomy."

Jim sits in the other room, chasing down a half-pint of Smirnoff with a Killian's Irish Red. Too sensitive for his own good, he is a writer, my former professor. My father's summation of him is dead-on. Alcohol only makes Jim feel more, and if he catches me talking so bluntly about him, he might launch into a rant. Or just the opposite and begin to cry. It's more than just the beer and the vodka that's making him so emotionally reckless. Our love for each other has proven devastating. He's left his family to start a new life with me. No matter how miserable things may have been at home, the guilt and the shame for selfishly thinking about his own future happiness over theirs are undoing him in painful ways. He sees himself as a bad husband, a bad father. My father knows better than anyone how a man has to bottom out before he can rebuild.

He laughs at my lobotomy crack. Sarcasm has always been our private language. It's how we reach out to each other.

"Okay, okay. Just promise me you won't get knocked-up. You'll get your degree first. As soon as a woman gets barefoot and pregnant, she's vulnerable."

My father is proud that I've been accepted to graduate school where I'll earn a Masters of Fine Arts degree. At this point in time I'm only twenty-nine and changing careers. Instead of high school with its juvenile detention slips and parent/teacher conferences, I'll be covering Chekhov, Hemingway, and Morrison to adults in college. Not only am I the child that stayed after my mother left, I'm also the one who has followed in his footsteps by pursuing an education. I'll be the first professor in the family.

My father talks like he knows something I don't, and it bothers me. He couldn't be more wrong.

"Who said I wanted a kid, anyway? Jim already has three. Don't worry, Dad. I'm off the hook."

Just as I'm hanging up, Jim comes into the room. He shakes his head.

"Why don't you ever say goodbye? He's your father."

"We never do. It's just our way."

How we speak to each other may be unclear to Jim. But I'm only too aware of the change in my father's voice and what I've just done by making him this promise. By breaking away from my father, I'm somehow breaking him. Many would argue he's been broken for some time, both financially and morally. Over a million dollars of his clients' money is missing. What can be accounted for had been invested in speculative ventures, undeveloped property in Hawaii and Nevada, a horse farm in Tennessee, thirteen purebreds, all in my father's name to "protect his clients from liability."

The State Bar Review Board didn't buy it and in revoking his license, a generous judge found my father had "committed acts of moral turpitude," instead of calling it for what it is: embezzlement. After I read the ruling on the State Bar's website, I looked up the word "turpitude" in the dictionary and found beside the definition synonyms like "vileness, depravity, shame." For any more information it suggested I look up the word "evil." My father maintains he did nothing improper. He had power of attorney. Although I have my doubts, I know for certain his conduct was no more or less moral than other lawyers who distort the truth to suit their own ends.

For better or worse I am a shyster's daughter and regardless of my father's guilt, I will defend him.

Even now, after years of struggling to come to terms with what happened that night, his phone call replays over and over in my head. He expected me to keep my promise of not getting pregnant, but unlike his word, mine can always be trusted. His timing can't be ignored. What he saw as a wake-up call is a warning of another kind. In less than eight hours after that phone call, my father was found dead.

PRISON WITHOUT WALLS

I am twelve years old when Kevin Cooper escapes from the California Institution for Men less than three miles from our home. That it is late and a school night doesn't matter. My mother is six months pregnant, and I help her drag our royal-sized dining room chairs in front of the sliders, blocking the glass with lumbering wood. Of course these heavy chairs will not stop him. But they may slow him down and give us those few seconds to either get out of the house or give my father time to aim.

My father is outside in his T-shirt and boxers, barefoot, yet armed with a hunting rifle. He checks the front and back doors, and inspects the garage, to make sure it holds nothing more than his diesel Mercedes and our Schwinn bicycles.

On the loose for less than seventy-two hours, Cooper is already suspected of bludgeoning a family in the hills. The carnage, the bodies, the blood, are all too grisly for the local networks to show. We only hear the details, which somehow makes them worse. Cooper has used a knife and hatchet. These are hands-on murders, the personal kind, though Cooper is a stranger to this family.

We see his mug shot—a black man in an orange prison jumpsuit with the start of dreadlocks springing from his head. I've seen enough prison photos from the files my father brings home to know that Cooper's smirk is nothing more than a pose. What I see is the face of a coward.

A weakling who rapes a woman with a screwdriver against her throat.

He is no man.

My mother must see it too because she turns off the TV. Her face is pale but it's always that way against her dark hair.

We live in a ranch-style home surrounded by oleander bushes, perfect for hiding.

My mother parts the curtains.

"He could be watching us right now," she says.

At age forty, her pregnancy is high-risk in more ways than one. An accident, she and my father say, but I know having another child is a last ditch effort at keeping our family together. My older sister and I are no longer enough.

It was my father's idea to move us from L.A. to Chino. He's moved his law practice too. A change is supposed to do us good.

"An alarm should've sounded," my father says, coming back into the house. His shoulders are nearly as wide as the doorway, and his neck is as thick as a linebacker, which he was, having once been recruited to play for Stanford. My father is not a man to be messed with. "It's supposed to go off every fifteen minutes when someone's escaped."

My mother laughs at this, at him, and places a protective hand over the hard mound of her belly.

"Who's supposed to hear it? Other prisoners?"

"What the hell kind of comment is that?" The gun lags at my father's side. "I'm doing my best."

"I know, Paul. I know. While that sick son of a bitch is hacking up me and the girls, you can hand him your card. He'll need a slick pro like you to spare him from the chair."

* * *

On that first night I sleep between my parents. Too frightened to stay, my sister Rhea is given permission to visit some family friends in San Diego. Sixteen and with a driver's license, it's easier on my parents if they just let her go. The house feels empty without her, consumed with the sound of my father's snoring that even the tissue crammed into my ears doesn't muffle.

Leaning against his side of the bed is his .300 Savage, fully loaded. If I reach over I can touch the cool barrel.

My father is a generic lawyer, taking on everything from divorces to drug offenses. I doubt if he is a good shot, considering he only hunts on occasional trips to Wyoming or Montana with one of his clients, the business ones, the ones he courts—like the handsome restaurateur from Bel Air who used to cart me on his back, table to table, making the candle-lit rounds, checking on things in the kitchen, until one night during dessert he returned me to my family's table, my breath smelling of wine from my first tasting, a trace of white dust in the man's dark mustache. Months later, his mind spun from all the cocaine and alcohol, he rolled his Jeep into a sand dune and never came out from the wreckage. My father also represents criminals and typically visits them behind the safety of bulletproof glass.

As I lie in bed, I think of the boy, a few years younger than me, who the night before lay awake in his parents' bedroom—only his mom and dad weren't sleeping. They were dead. His sister and a neighbor friend who was sleeping over had been murdered, too. They were ambushed in their sleep by a man with a hatchet in one hand, a knife in the other.

The boy was stabbed in the chest. He was stabbed in the head. Then his throat was slit. The only way he made it through the night, the eleven hours it took until help found him, was by plugging four fingers in the slash to stop the bleeding. He was airlifted to ICU at Loma Linda Hospital. I wonder who's sitting with him now while he fights to breathe. How hard it must be for him to want to live, knowing the rest of his family has been killed.

* * *

The next morning at school, there is no talk of Cooper's escape. Yet the door to the classroom isn't propped open with a doorstop. Instead Mrs. Lincoln pulls on it after the first bell, making sure it's locked. None of us are allowed to use the restroom by ourselves. Not even with a buddy system. We have to be accompanied to and from there in a small group by the teacher's aide.

Recess is on a rainy day schedule, as if it's not clear and warm outside. After lunch, we sit on the floor in the multi-purpose room and watch the animated mice movie, *The Rescuers.*

When we return to the classroom, we're stuck watching another film. This one is very different. We needed to get our parents' signatures for it. The boys are sent to Mr. Kroger's class to watch their own. The movie is actually a slide show with a drawing of a woman; her insides are reduced to a wide tube that leads to two narrow pouches on either side of her hips. These are her ovaries.

Mrs. Lincoln flips the slide. It's the same drawing, only now there's a tiny circle with a curvy tail in the middle of the woman's tube. Mrs. Lincoln narrates from a stapled packet.

"The sperm swims up the canal and breaks through the woman's egg, fertilizing it. A man and woman have intercourse when they want to produce a child."

In the next slide, the egg has suddenly come to life and bats a set of long eyelashes. The tiny head of the sperm grows a face and puckers up for a whistle.

All the girls giggle, except for me.

I picture something else. I picture my parents naked in bed, my father sweating and heaving on top of my mother, purposely releasing microscopic live things hidden in slime. While my sister and I may not have seen them, we heard them in our room late one night at the Desert Rose Hotel in Palm Springs when they thought we were asleep. We heard our father's heavy grunts, our mother's thin cries. He was smothering her in the sheets. When I tried to get up out of bed to help her, Rhea pinched my ear hard and whispered that I needed to go back to sleep. It was no big deal. Mom was all right. They were just making a baby.

Apparently it's an act of love. It's called making love, having sex. In time it will no longer sicken me. It will be something I'll want to do when I'm older, when I'm in love. But as I sit listening at my desk, even in Mrs. Lincoln's clinical terms, it still sounds unclean.

My mother seems dirty for letting my father do that to her, especially since they spend most of the time arguing.

After the slide show, Mrs. Lincoln informs us about our monthly friend who will likely appear in the next year or so. She holds up a small cylinder of cotton with a string and instructs us on how best to insert the plastic applicator so that after its removal, what's left inside will soak up the blood.

My best friend Tomoko makes a face at me. Although she's Asian, her mother tells her she's a Japanese girl before she's anything else. We're not allowed to play at each other's houses, not because I'm Greek, but because I'm white. Her mother doesn't see the difference. Tomoko's hair is hard to manage, so her mother braids it into two thick pigtails. This style doesn't make her feel very pretty, so at recess she'll take a couple of tiny white flowers from the weeds in the grass and tuck them behind one ear.

She points at Mrs. Lincoln and the dangling tampon.

"We have to leave that inside our vagina?" She mouths this part of our anatomy as if it's something secretive, something bad.

I shrug and pretend that the idea doesn't panic me.

"Guess so," I say. "It's better than wearing a miniature diaper."

When school lets out, we're still in lockdown mode, and my mother must waddle through the entrance and past the administrative offices and upper grade playground to Mrs. Lincoln's room to pick me up.

My mother wears a T-shirt with the word "baby" and an arrow pointing downward in neutral yellow, just below her breasts. Neither of my parents wants to find out the baby's sex. It will be a surprise, as if my mother getting pregnant isn't enough of one for the family. She smiles self-consciously because of the slight space between her front teeth or maybe she's reacting to me. Although I try and smile back, I wind up looking somewhere else. It's impossible not to be embarrassed by her big belly, that hardened hump of proof she and my father had sex.

* * *

The bedtime ritual doesn't change once my sister is forced to return home a week and a half later. My father puts her to work placing the rest of the dining room chairs against the other slider, the one in our parents' bedroom. That's how Cooper entered his victims' home—through an open slider. For forty-eight hours he had camped out in the abandoned house next door.

He was in no hurry. Running too fast is how most escaped convicts are caught. If he stayed in Chino long enough, he knew the cops would figure he was farther away and stop looking for him here. He was patient and smart about it because he'd done this before. Using his prison contacts, my father learns Cooper had escaped a year earlier from a psychiatric ward in Pennsylvania. Cooper had gotten a real California driver's license under an alias and had been arrested under this false name. He faked an illness too, so he could be transferred to a minimum security prison.

With a manual bicycle pump, my father inflates the mattress we use for camping. My sister will sleep at the foot of the bed.

"This is stupid," she complains, pushing the last of the chairs against the glass. Her face is plastered salmon pink in Calamine lotion to avoid breakouts. "He's long gone to Mexico or Siberia by now."

My parents' bed is big, a California King, and I climb up on it and slide under the covers. I'm getting used to sleeping between them, and I like how it's my presence that helps them get along better.

"How do you know he's gone?" I ask.

My sister doesn't bother answering and instead looks for support from our mother, her strongest ally.

"The cops found that family's station wagon in Long Beach. There's no way he's . . ."

My father pulls out the pump, adds a couple puffs of his own air, then plugs the hole.

"Enough, Rhea."

He drops the air mattress and it skids at her feet, looking more like it should be floating out on the pool than resting on the bedroom floor.

My mother stays quiet. She is too uncomfortable, too pregnant, to argue about something as trivial as sleeping arrangements. Sleeping through the entire night is her only objective. She props up three pillows where she'll doze off practically upright. If she lies flat, the baby's bulk cuts off her air.

A tall glass of ice water sweats on the nightstand. Lately, she can't drink enough liquids, and sometimes in the middle of the night I hear her getting up to fill her glass at the tap in the bathroom. She'll stand at the sink and down it in a couple gulps, then refill the glass before returning to bed.

As she stretches a sheet over the mattress, my sister groans loud, exaggerated groans. Where did her fear go? The fear that sent her crying and stuffing clothes in a duffel, insisting she be allowed to stay someplace else. Cooper's escape was just an excuse to get away from our own house for a while.

"She's right, Paul," my mother finally says. "We probably should let the girls sleep in their rooms."

My father clicks on the safety of his Savage and looks at my mother as if she's betrayed him somehow. It's the way he always looks at her when she sides with my sister.

Sometimes it feels like we're on opposing teams—my father and I left with no other choice but to pick each other. We've always been the odd men out, and, as a consequence, he has raised me as both his son and daughter. He has taught me how to throw a baseball, straight and hard, and every summer he buys us season tickets, and together we sit drinking Cokes, cracking peanut shells and cheering on the Angels at Anaheim Stadium.

"Give it a couple more nights, June." My father says this with the kind of care and caution that makes it clear who he's really protecting. But he can't ever keep me safe. I know this now. I know that no amount of locks on the doors, chairs at the glass, or rifles by the bed will change the fact that we're defenseless in our sleep.

The boy is going to make it, he's going to survive.

This news told to me again and again does nothing to rid the image I see every night of him left for dead on the floor of his parents' bedroom—wide-eyed in his struggle to keep the life from leaking out of him between his fingers.

My mother turns out the light, my sister squeaks around on the air mattress, fidgeting to get comfortable.

My father settles on his side, settling in for some raucous snoring.

In the dark, my eyes snap open. This is when he comes, just as he would much later in life, for my father—that *malaka* in the guise of a black ski mask and gloves. I'm the only one in the family who is still spooked by the bogeyman.

THE FIRST SOUNDS OF FAMILY

I should be suspicious a few weeks later when my sister asks right after dinner if I'd like to go get ice cream. She never asks me to go anywhere, never even comes out of her room. Despite the statewide manhunt for Cooper, our parents have allowed her back in her own bed at night. It's not like she's busy on the phone, talking boys with friends. She doesn't have any. Ever since we moved to Chino, she keeps more and more to herself. She misses too much school because she's tired. And the few friends she did make have all but given up calling to find out what's wrong. My parents now pay a shrink in L.A. to figure out what they can't.

As I reach the car I call shotgun, forgetting in my excitement that I'm to be the only passenger.

We ride in her 280-Z, my father's old sports car. It was a gift for having aced her driver's test. The car is intended to be an incentive for her to drive to school, providing her with another kind of license—to show off. Before accepting it, she insisted that the maroon car be painted white like the Z the cool photographer drives in Madonna's "Borderline" video.

My sister takes me to Baskin Robbins and buys me a double scoop of chocolate chip. For some reason she doesn't give me time to eat it there. Never before has she let me eat or drink in her beloved car.

I hang behind in the store, convinced this is some sort of trap.

"Are you sure?"

Rhea has the lightest colored eyes in the family. They're hazel, and they change colors depending upon the light in them. Something dark is in them now, something deliberate and dead set that's doing more than clouding her judgment.

"C'mon, Paula," she says. "Let's just go."

On the way out, I grab a wad of napkins.

Instead of returning home, she speeds south down Central Avenue, toward the outskirts of the city. We pass Chino Grain and Feed built like a gigantic aluminum shed, where my parents pick up bales of hay and straw for the horses. We pass the grass field and wooden bleachers that is the Chino Fairgrounds. I don't like where we're headed. The prison is less than a block away.

"Where are we going?"

"I told you. We're going on a drive." She looks over at me in disgust. "It's dripping." My sister no longer likes food. She used to be overweight, so overweight that our grandmother, our yia yia, would sew her polyester pants with an elastic waist. In the last six months, she's dropped more than fifty pounds. Now too thin, her weight still eats at her in other ways, and she subsists on nothing but Diet Coke and Cup o' Noodles.

Quickly, I lick around the sides of the cone and stare out the window. The prison is surrounded by chain link, which is how it got its nickname "the prison with no walls." Barbed wire coils across the top, though Cooper didn't risk climbing over it and cutting up his hands. He didn't have to. According to my father, he walked right out through a hole in the fence. "Either he cut it himself or somebody else had before him," my father explained. "Naturally, they're trying to keep that part out of the papers."

All of the front towers are unlit, except for one where a man in a dark gray baseball cap is visible. Even at this distance, I can tell he isn't looking where he should be. He's focused on something inside the tower, maybe watching a baseball game or a game show on one of those portable TV's.

I lean toward the dash and point at the guard.

"How come he isn't on the lookout? He's watching TV, I can tell. Don't you see him?"

My sister bats my arm out of her line of sight.

"He's probably watching the monitors, Paula."

At the stoplight, she turns right, in the direction of the hills, and there is now no denying where she is taking us. I roll down the window. The night air blows hard and fast in my face, and I can't catch my breath. Ice cream melts cold down my fingers. I toss out the cone, hoping a cop will see it and cite her a thousand bucks for littering. Anything to make her stop.

The 280-Z doesn't have power steering and she needs both hands to make this next sharp turn. There are no streetlights so I'm not sure how she knows this is the right road. It's made of dirt and gravel, and at the sound of the spoiler scraping the ground, I'm convinced she'll change her mind and back right down. Instead she downshifts into first gear and steps harder on the gas.

Hurriedly, I roll up the window, as if being separated by glass is an actual form of protection.

"Turn around," I say. "*Please, Rhea.*"

"You need to confront your fears." Her tone is polished, adult sounding, possibly like her new L.A. shrink.

The house is just a dark bulky shape and I tell myself my sister might've gotten the addresses mixed up. This house could belong to a family that is off on vacation or simply out to the movies. The front yard is in need of trimming.

She stops the car in the circular driveway and outstretches her arm as if she's performed a magic trick.

"You see? Nobody's here."

If this isn't the spot where the worst mass murder in San Bernardino County took place, others have apparently made the same mistake as my sister. Beer bottles and fast food wrappers litter the front yard. Less than a couple of months, the house has become a creepy hangout spot for teenagers. It seems too soon. The cops should've secured it longer, but there's no trace they were even here. No yellow police tape sealing shut the front doors or fingerprint dust around the windows and door knobs. No obvious signs of the bloody slaughter that occurred inside.

Cooper attacked the father first because he was the strongest, an ex-Marine who would've fought back on instinct. He stabbed and struck the father's head and chest so many times that one of the man's fingers was later found inside the closet. Next, Cooper turned the knife and hatchet on the wife who only got as far as the foot of the bed. The children, awakening to her screams, must've run toward the bedroom where Cooper hid like a shadow in the dark.

"I want to go home *now*," I say.

"Or else what?"

My sister is taunting me by bringing me here. It has nothing to do with overcoming my fears. All she wants is to scare me.

Maybe it's my anger that forces me out of the car and makes me grab an empty beer can. Although the lip of it is too smooth to do any real damage, I have a plan. The tab twists off easily and there it is, a tiny, jagged stump. I hold it against the car door, the custom paint job that my father jokingly said cost him an early appearance in L.A. Superior Court with a perverted high school gym teacher. The man was caught, his silk running shorts around his ankles, in the backseat of his Prelude during lunch period with a seventeen-year-old girl. Luckily for him, the student thought she was in love and clammed up. My father got the charges dropped, arguing that although he exercised poor judgment, the gym teacher did nothing criminally wrong by showing this girl how to avoid a groin pull.

I rattle my threat for effect.

"A long curly swirl would look cool," I say. "Or maybe my name in cursive."

Even in the dark, I think I see her eyes change color.

"You little *skatofatsa.*"

Cursing me in Greek, calling me a shitface, is just a start. Part of me is scared because I could be in for a serious beating. Sometimes she play fights with me, getting too rough, and I wind up locking myself in my room, hating her, with a reddened cheek or a welt on my forearm. It occurs to me that my sister might even ditch me here on Cooper's murdering ground.

"Don't think I won't do it," I warn, thinking up my own Greek curse word I've heard my father use. "From taillight to headlight, *palio hondree.*"

I'm not sure what I've called her. My father shouted those two words once on our way back from an Angels' game when we were cut off on the freeway by a female driver. They are successful in getting a reaction out of my sister. She reaches into the glove compartment, pops a pill from a prescription bottle, and downs it with a gulp of Diet Coke. I've only seen her take medication if she has a cold. This is different, and I worry if what she's just swallowed is going to make her sleepy. Already, she looks worn out.

"Christ," she says. "Just get in."

I wait until we're safely back on Central before I dare ask what I called her.

My sister smiles, though it's an uneasy one. The pill has relaxed her some.

"You called me a fat ass."

The worst I've ever yelled at her is *vlaka*. Moron is nothing compared to what I just said.

"Sorry," I say. "You're not fat." And although I mean it, my apology comes too late.

For a moment my sister is lost in thought, busily adding up how many more calories she'll have to subtract from her diet, one less Styrofoam package of soup, one more can of Diet Coke to bloat fullness in her belly. It will be my unintentional insult that starves her to the bone.

* * *

"Something's wrong with Mom." Rhea changes the subject. "They think she has diabetes." Hearing this scares me as much as having seen the outside of that family's house. The real reason why my sister took me out for ice cream was to break the news that our mother is sick.

"How do you know?"

"I heard them talking."

"How'd she get it?"

"It's not like it's contagious. She got it from being pregnant. It's taken too much out of her. She's not exactly young, you know."

"Is she going to be okay?"

My sister nods and takes another sip of Diet Coke. On average she'll finish two six packs of diet soft drinks plus the fountain kind she picks up in drive thrus per day.

"She just needs to see the doctor more until the baby comes."

"She's carrying it low."

"So?"

"They say high if it's a girl, low if it's a boy."

"Who's they?"

"I learned it in health class," I lie. Truth is I listened to Mrs. Lincoln and Miss Marks, the teacher's aide, talking softly after we came in from lunch recess, when we were supposed to have our heads on our desks, taking a rest. "Besides," I add. "Men Dad's age have a low sperm count. All he has left are the male swimmers."

Rhea seems disinterested, maybe even a little disturbed by what I've learned.

"I want another sister," mine says.

In shame I look out the window, even staying quiet as we pass the prison, because I know she means it.

* * *

To waste time while my mother is in the doctor's office, I play Frogger, a miniature electronic arcade game. She has been in there long enough for me to reach the third level, one I've never gotten to before. The digital logs shoot out fast, and there are no lily pads to jump onto for safety. Within a few seconds I've let two frogs drown before my finger even presses the "hop" button.

Finally, my mother appears while I'm on my last frog life. The doctor has escorted her to the waiting area, which I know is a bad sign. Usually that job is left for one of his assistants. Dr. Simpkins is old, long past retirement age, probably in his early seventies, and I imagine his age shows the most in his hands. At this stage in his life they're meant for simple tasks like holding onto a fishing pole off the Florida Keys or pulling down the handle of a slot machine in Laughlin, Nevada. They're no longer meant for something as delicate and urgent as reaching into a woman's body to help guide out a new life.

The game beeps indicating the loss of my last frog life, and quickly I turn it off.

My mother's hands cover her face and her body heaves so hard from crying that her shirt rides up. Something slick and gooey is visible on the bottom of her belly.

Without thinking, I leap out of my chair at Dr. Simpkins.

"What did you do to her?"

Yelling at an adult is wrong, but sending my mother into hysterics isn't right either.

Awkwardly, with her belly between us, she holds me by the shoulders.

"Don't raise your voice, Paula." Her reprimand is weaker than her touch. The last thing I want to do is upset her even more, so I listen. Purposely, after I retrieve my game from the chair, I wedge myself between her and Dr. Simpkins.

He hands her a slip of paper, a prescription order, probably a new medication to treat her diabetes.

"They'll be expecting you at seven in the morning on Monday," he informs her.

Dr. Simpkins pats her on the back, a swift show of consolation before closing the door and moving on to his next appointment.

As my mother stares at the slip before stashing it in her purse, I'm able to make out enough of the doctor's scribbling to see it's not a prescription for medication. Instructions are written down for the hospital's technician to *Check for demise of fetus.*

"He's dead?"

This comes out before I consider what it will do to my mother. I'm only thinking of myself, my own hurt, how my little brother, and I'm sure it's my baby brother, might be gone before I ever get a chance to meet him. My father and I have big plans. In a couple years, when he's old enough, he'll fill the third seat at all the Angels' home games. I will teach him how to throw, how to catch and how to bat like Rod Carew and heavy hitter Brian Downing. I think of my mother and how she's spent her entire pregnancy decorating his room in yellows, not just because it's a neutral color, but also because it's a cheerful one. I think of how it took my father half a day to figure out the directions to put together the new crib. Just yesterday my sister helped my mother string up the safari mobile—little stuffed zebras, lions, and giraffes hanging by invisible string. The changing table is equipped with baby powder, cloth diapers, and Baby Magic lotion. Our home smells and feels like my baby brother already lives in it.

Her strength has returned because my mother hugs me hard.

"We don't know yet. Dr. Simpkins couldn't hear a heartbeat. He said it's a possibility."

"So he's making us go home, not knowing?"

"There's nothing more he can do."

There's plenty more he could do. He could admit her into the hospital. They could run the test right now and find out. Sending her home, not knowing if she's carrying around a dead baby, is cruel.

By the time we reach the car, my mother stops crying, and even insists on stopping off at 7-11 for my favorite dinosaur egg jawbreaker as my reward for having to wait so long at the doctor's. When we get home, my father is still at the office, and she secludes herself in their bedroom where she'll rest until dinner.

My sister and I are in charge of making it and she actually comes out of her room without threat or force. I boil pasta for spaghetti and my sister chops tomato, carrots, and red cabbage to make a salad. Something stops me from telling her what happened at the doctor's, how our brother or sister may be dead. Guiltily, I like making dinner with her, and if I say anything she'll want to comfort my mother and they'll freeze me out.

Tonight, instead of eating in the dining room, we set up at the kitchen table. Before my father has a chance to finish his salad, my mother breaks the news that Dr. Simpkins couldn't hear the baby's heartbeat.

My father refuses to believe it. In his line of work, there's almost always a catch, a way out.

His reaction is exactly what she's expecting and her face visibly tires.

"He tried a couple of times, Paul."

"Well, he didn't try hard enough." My father stuffs a forkful of pasta in his mouth, ignoring the rest of his salad. "That deaf old man probably couldn't hear his own heart with a stethoscope."

Nobody else at the table seems so convinced, though my mother lets it drop. Rhea serves herself a plate of what we're eating. Of course, she's eating the spaghetti noodles plain, no Prego sauce, not even melted butter or olive oil. My mother nudges her plate of spaghetti away but forces down a glass of whole milk, hopeful the baby still might need the calcium.

Worry has taken over all of us. It keeps us in the same room when usually, after dinner, we scatter. Instead of sprawling out on the family room floor, just inches from the TV, the way my father always does right after dinner, he sits on the couch beside my mother. One arm is behind her on the cushion, and he gently rubs her neck. With the other, he holds out the remote, channel surfing. Rhea collapses on a black and white polka dotted beanbag she brought in from her room, and I take a couch pillow and lay belly down on the floor.

My father decides on *Magnum P.I.*, my mother's favorite show because it takes place in Hawaii. We'd planned a trip there this summer before we learned my mother's due date is in late September.

Halfway through the program, Kevin Cooper's face suddenly appears on screen. It's the same mug shot my mother and I saw the night we first heard he escaped. She turns up the sound.

"Paul."

There's no need for her to call out to him since he's just in the kitchen, right next to the family room, and he can hear everything.

The female reporter is standing in front of a jail in Santa Barbara where Cooper has been arrested for raping a woman at knife point. My father comes back into the room, leaving the bag of popcorn he'd just popped in the microwave. After two months of running, Cooper has been captured. He was working as a deckhand for a couple and their five-year-old girl, with whom he'd sailed from Ensenada, Mexico, to Pelican Cove, just off Santa Barbara.

"I told you people he ran to Mexico," my sister pronounces.

What she says isn't what makes us laugh. We laugh for other reasons. We laugh in relief that Cooper's finally been caught. We laugh that we'll no longer have to blockade our sliders with big dining room chairs. We laugh at the awful dinner we just ate. We laugh at how I boiled the noodles for too long, how we didn't even need to eat them with a fork since they stuck together in clumps like finger food. We laugh at how all of us ate the salad Rhea made even though she forgot the dressing.

My mother holds her belly and that's when she cries out she feels it, buried deep inside the womb, the baby roused and agitated by the first sounds of family.

WHAT THEY TOLD ME AFTER HE DIED

I turned your father down three times for a date. I had to. He was a football star and girls gave him anything he wanted. First he asked me when we were at a dance, then after he ran into me with my girlfriends at the drive-in. Finally, at the park while I was practicing with my drill team, he got my attention by nearly ramming into the fender of my powder blue M.G.

It was the way he apologized that got to me. Both of us were sorry it had come to that.

—June Priamos, ex-wife

I don't care what anybody tells me. That stripper chick was in on it. You don't get it. I *know* she was.

—Rhea Priamos

Your father showed up here once with a real pretty girl. Sorry, I can't remember her name. She reminded me of Halle Berry. Smooth skin, short dark hair. He couldn't take his eyes off her. Man, neither could I.

—Luis Martinez, manager of Boca Grande

You watch out for Gil. I mean it. With your father gone, there's no telling what he's capable of. He wanted your father's approval like he wanted your pappou's. He never got either. How could he? Everybody knows he's a psychopath. You know what he said while standing over his own father's grave? "How long will it take before the maggots come."

Nobody said a word. Maybe they were too shocked, so I told him, "Apparently not long. One's already here."

—June Priamos

It's not uncommon to begin the embalming procedures on the same day the deceased is brought in, especially if requested by the family.

—Antonio Sanchez, funeral director at Chapel of Remembrance

THE INSANITY DEFENSE

My brother is born all yellow like his room. Two weeks overdue and with a bad case of jaundice, he is extracted from my mother's body with the help of giant metallic tongs and a scalpel. By this time even her liver wants him out because it's stopped cleaning red blood cells. Only my father is able to watch the birth. My mother is out cold.

Nicholas weighs in at nine pounds even with a tuft of dark wet hair and puffy little hands. My sister and I catch a glimpse of him from behind the glass in the nursery. The nurse cradles him as if we should be impressed. But his face is still unrecognizable, still swollen and squished from fitting for so long inside the walls of our mother's uterus. His ears are pointy like Dr. Spock's, and his tiny mouth is twisted in terror at being cut out and cut from her body. He's my baby brother.

"He looks like an alien baby," I say.

My sister shrugs me off. She doesn't seem too concerned that our new brother is sick. It bothers me enough for both of us. Two other babies, two healthy babies are red-faced and squirming in their plastic bubble basinets. Especially under the fluorescents, I can see that Nicholas is the wrong color.

"I hope Mom's okay," Rhea says turning toward the hall. "Dad shouldn't be the only one who gets to see her."

Neither of my surviving grandparents is at the hospital. My mother didn't want my yia yia or Uncle Gil here. Can't say I blame her. Yia Yia's face could scare the life out of any newborn. Her wrinkles are deep and unforgiving, from a lifetime of holding grudges. She was widowed young at forty-four; her husband fifteen years her senior had been hand-picked by her father one summer on a trip to the islands. Their love was learned, practiced over time through the birth and raising of three boys. But his heart was bad and when he was taken from Yia Yia too soon, it made her old and bitter beyond her years. This is how my mother explained it to me one night after she caught me dipping into her Oil of Olay night cream, slopping it all over my cheeks and forehead. Since I was half Greek, I figured I'd better start early, seeing I stood a fifty-fifty chance of one day looking like my yia yia.

In order to be fair and avoid my father sulking, my mother also didn't ask her mother to be present for the birth. Both of their fathers passed early, my mother's father from cirrhosis of the liver and my father's from a heart attack. "It's a man's job to provide for his family, then die before retirement," my father often says, usually when paying the bills.

He appears from behind the swinging doors. The paper booties he wore in the operating room still cover up his dress shoes. This morning he had been called out of a bail hearing after my mother's water broke.

"Have you seen Nicholas?"

My brother is named after our Greek grandfather, our pappou, a man my father still mourns decades later at holidays, especially Christmas. Pappou delivered more than fresh fruit to the Central Market in downtown L.A. for his wealthy brother-in-law who owned a produce company. He delivered the best one-liners that kept his family both in hysterics and in check. He had a practical habit of using a bar of Ivory soap on his head full of white hair, claiming the suds were why he never went bald, a habit my father eventually picked up. But what pappou is known best for is the time he grew desperate at the thought of his un-married youngest son at twenty-three still living at the house. Somehow he snowed Helena Stamapolous, the bright young daughter of a family friend, into marrying Gil by telling her that a boy who never strays far from home is one who will never stray from his wife.

My mother doesn't even get to choose Nicholas's middle name because he's named after my father. Obviously, I am too, with just an added vowel attached at the end.

"How's Mom." Rhea says this more like an accusation than a ques-tion, as if our father is to blame for the birth being forced and unnatural.

My father sneaks a look at the other babies, maybe hoping his own will somehow be lying in a plastic bubble on wheels too instead of where he really is, his tiny vitals all wired up in an incubator.

"She's fine, but she won't come to for another hour or so."

Rhea takes a seat. When the news hit, she was pulled out of first period at her new school, a Christian academy in La Verne. She tells our parents she likes it, but she tells them a lot of things she doesn't mean. She tells them she eats too, and I've caught her twice tossing out the noodles, finishing only the broth.

"You two go," she decides for us. "I'll wait."

On the way home, my father pops a cassette in the tape deck. It isn't Pavorotti or even his favorite country singer, Eddie Rabbit. It's a foreign sounding voice, broken from nerves, from his Middle Eastern accent. It's the voice of Bared Garrata, my father's client, who has just been arrested for murder. Intermittently, his voice is interrupted by the loud creak of an office chair, the interrogating cop leaning back. They never give the comfortable, reclining seat to the suspect.

"Again," the investigator states louder into the speaker, for the record. "You're waiving your right to counsel."

There's mumbling and then Bared blurts out, "I have no choice. I have to shoot."

"Bullshit," my father says. "You hear that, Paula Girl?" He points to the cassette player. "That's exactly the place where I can get this tossed out. He's a goddamn foreigner. He's not even sure what they're saying."

I've heard this man's confession before, and I find that part hard to believe. His English sounds crystal clear to me. It's my father's first homicide and he's played the tape countless times since the murder occurred. He's moving up in the legal world, from the DUIs and drug offenses, where nobody pays much attention, to a murder that has made the local paper in Orange County. Even the birth of his first son can't stop my father from thinking about the case, debating whether he should try and get the confession thrown out or use it toward an insanity defense. Either way, my father is behind the eight ball. The hearing earlier today was for Bared and because he holds dual citizenship in Armenia, a country that is considered by many to be the northern extension of the Middle East, bail is set at half a million.

Bared works as an assistant manager at a fan manufacturing plant in the city of Orange. He is not a terrorist. Neither is he a religious zealot. He is a family man with two daughters and an American wife. One afternoon Bared is set off when he's convinced he overhears subordinates and his boss laughing in the break room about his small penis.

He must not be able to sexually satisfy his fair-skinned wife, they say. She needs a white man or a Mexican or Black, like them.

The next morning Bared shows up at work, walks right into his boss's office and fires one shot, square in the chest. The bullet blows clear through, burying in the back of the dead man's chair. Security doesn't tackle Bared on his way out of the building because he never runs. There are no other casualties since the act, as he sees it, has little to do with violence. He is defending his manhood, defending his marriage. Talk of pleasuring another man's wife in his culture calls for immediate and unrelenting measures. After the shooting, Bared leaves the weapon by the body and waits in his office where he phones his wife, explaining that something has come up. Save him a plate. He won't make it home in time for dinner.

My father wants to argue that the voices Bared heard are really his own, that he's a paranoid schizophrenic and needs psychological help, not incarceration.

"He isn't crazy," I say. "You'd better come up with something else."

We're almost home and out on his front porch, I see Moses Murillo, our neighbor, dousing the grass with his own brand of weed killer, a can of gasoline. He's chosen the worst possible time to pour flammable liquid on his yard, considering it's early fall and everything is still hot and dry from summer and the Santa Anas have already begun to stir.

But nothing Moses does ever makes any sense. He's a Vietnam War vet with irrational moods that must make his family want to duck from the swing. Even with the windows closed, we can sometimes hear him yelling at his two boys with the kind of rage that has made my parents anonymously call the cops more than once. In the Murillos' one acre backyard stands a baseball diamond with real bases and a pitcher's

mound, and by the time the police arrive, Moses will be crouched behind home plate, catching his sons Cheech and Rigo's slow pitches,
patiently instructing them how to improve their throw. Moses used to
beat on his dog too, a beautiful German Shepherd named Dexter, until
my father convinced him to sell it for big bucks to a client of his who
owned a guard dog business.

I point to Moses.

"Now that's crazy."

My father chuckles and waves. In response, Moses lifts up the gas
can like he's making a champagne toast.

Bared's rambling confession is still playing as we pull into our
driveway. "They want to take her from me. He say they sleep with my
wife. I buy handgun for two hundred dollars. A Filipino man, by bakery.
Say it's okay, I buy for protection. Those people, they insult me, they
come for my family."

The cop grills Bared some more, getting him to admit he purchased the stolen gun the night before the shooting off of some gang
bangers while cruising the streets of Artesia. He conceals the gun in his
Tupperware lunch box.

"What makes you think he's sane?" my father asks.

He sounds irritated at hearing the prosecutor's likely argument out
of his twelve-and-a-half-year-old daughter.

I'm surprised he's even listening, and I open the car door, sorry I
brought it up.

"He sounds too nervous," I say. "You can hear it in his voice. He
knows what he did is wrong."

At dusk, my father orders me out of my room to go and feed the
horses. Through the chain link fences, I can see Rigo and Cheech are

still out playing ball. Rigo's at the plate and Cheech is pitching. Overpowering the hard pop of a Louisville Slugger or the even harder punch of a caught ball is the electric sound coming from the oleander bushes. Not to be mistaken for high tension wires, these are horse flies, a genetically pumped up version of the house variety, that buzz and bat against the leaves. It doesn't matter that they don't bite. They are dangerous in other ways. They live around horses, hoping to swarm on any scratch, laying eggs inside until the scratch turns into an infected flesh wound. If even one fly gets tangled in my hair, I'm petrified it might feast on my scalp, and I may just have to grab the horse clippers my mother keeps in the hay barn and the Murillo boys can watch me shave my head bald.

With my hands flying overhead, I rush down the steps, then stop before I reach the bottom so they don't see. The doors to the hay barn are latched yet unlocked. My horse, Boo Boo, an Arabian trail horse, whinnies and paces back and forth in his pipe corral. The other horse, named Lou, is a former prized Saddlebred. My father bought him for my mother on their first anniversary. The horse is too old now to do more than toss his head impatiently in front of his aluminum feeder.

I hear the two-fingered whistle, coming from one of the Murillo boys. My face feels hot and tight like it's sun burned, and all I can think to do is pretend they're not following my every move.

In order to scare off the mice, I kick the door a couple times, then pull off two pre-sliced flakes and balance them, one on each arm. I'm allergic to alfalfa, and if I'm not quick I'll wheeze like an asthmatic and my arms will rash up and itch. Just as I'm hoisting the flake into Boo Boo's feeder, something rustles in the alfalfa, something alive. At the first sight of gray fur, I drop the flake between the pipes, piercing the air with my squeal. The mouse scurries off into a puff of dirt.

Behind me, a Murillo boy laughs. I toss the other flake at a hungry Lou, and make a bee line for the house.

"Shut the hell up," Cheech shouts at his little brother.

* * *

I'm on the phone telling Tomoko what happened with the Murillo brothers when our call gets cut short, an emergency breakthrough from the Orange County prison. Whenever it's a collect call, I know to accept the charges. The client in jail will pay for it later, getting double-billed for calling collect, let alone our home number.

I've never spoken to a murderer before, and although my father slept with a hunting rifle by his side when Cooper had escaped, this killer is different. He's my father's front page client and I'll get into trouble if I'm not polite.

"May I speak with your father?" The precise way in which he forms each syllable makes him sound successful, like one of my father's business clients. Even murderers have phone manners.

"Just a second, please," I say.

My father is in the living room, the TV on, tuning out the ten o'clock news with the aid of a Walkman. He wears headphones, listening again no doubt to Bared's confession.

Scattered across the table are black and whites of the crime scene. One shot is of the victim's head thrown back against the chair, his eyes bulging. On the front of his shirt is a small hole where the bullet had entered, and I am shocked at how little blood there is.

I mouth Bared's name as I hand over the phone.

My father slides the headphones back a little to make room for the receiver. From his end I'm able to put together half the story. Bared has been roughed up at the jail. A broken nose and finger. It's race related. While being struck and kicked he heard somebody call him a sand nigger. At twelve I'd heard "nigger" used solely as an insult to a black person. In time I'll learn the offensive word will do even more damage being used as a root slur against all races.

My father promises that tomorrow he'll have pictures taken and will use them at the emergency bail hearing.

*   *   *

"The guards beat him up?" I ask after my father is done talking.

He hangs up and shrugs.

"Hard to tell. Usually it's the arresting cops. He looked fine this morning. Sometimes a client will do it to himself if he thinks an ass kicking will help get him out sooner."

I hear my sister unlocking the front door. She looks satisfied, refreshed, her lips abloom in bright fuchsia. She takes a long sip of her thirty-two ounce McDonald's cup, leaving no print.

"Mom finally woke up."

I wonder if our mother came around on her own or if Rhea helped.

My father removes the headset as if the foam parts impede his hearing.

"How is she?"

"They're releasing her tomorrow morning."

My father tosses the rest of the Walkman onto the coffee table.

"Goddamn it."

"That's one way of looking at it." My sister passes us in a burst of Poison, her favorite scent, getting his reaction all wrong.

My father shakes his head at the circumstances he can't change, at the toxic relationship the two of them share and how what just happened with Bared has ruined his chances of being the good husband. No matter how fast he is at the bail hearing, all my mother will see is that she's just given birth to his son and he's late in picking her up from the hospital.

* * *

The next morning I'm pouring a bowl of Honeynut Cheerios when my father knocks on Rhea's door, open handed. In his other hand is a cup of coffee.

"Time to get up," he calls at the closed door.

Though I should be going to school, my father has decided that I'm to go with him. He doesn't want to have to worry about picking me up after school. An emergency bail hearing has been granted. I'm not sure how my father is able to pull this off so soon, but he did and we're already late for it.

By the time I've finished the Cheerios and have bussed my bowl in the dishwasher, he's dressed in a suit and tie.

Dabs of toilet paper stick to the red nicks on his face where he cut himself shaving. He reeks of my mother's last Christmas present, Drakkar Noir. His open hand on my sister's door has turned into a fist.

"Get up *now*," he says. "I'm not paying nearly a grand a month for you to sleep away the semester."

My chest tightens at the beginnings of an argument, so I break in with the white flag.

"Okay, Dad," I say. "I think she heard you."

A couple of minutes later my sister emerges on her way to the bathroom. Her short hair is smashed along the side of her head where she's been sleeping, her face cracked in places with dried Calamine. From her skeletal shoulders, her nightgown hangs as if being held up by a wire hanger. She doesn't look herself and hasn't for some time. The pills her L.A. shrink prescribed aren't working.

Before she shuts the bathroom door, she faces our father dead on, calling up energy from down deep.

"Mom told me what you did to her."

Whatever Rhea claims he's done to our mother, it must be true because my father backs off. He snaps at me to get in the goddamn car and as we leave, it's anyone's guess if she'll make it to school or simply head back to bed.

* * *

Although my father is over forty and a good fifty pounds overweight, I have trouble keeping up with him in the courthouse halls. My Van slip-ons squeak at every turn on the shiny floors, grabbing the attention of a few men in suits who look a little puzzled at seeing me, a seventh grader, tagging along with her father to court. It's impossible to tell which of the men are attorneys and which are cleaned up drug dealers, murderers and thieves.

Inside the gallery, my father seats me in the last row. The Drakkar Noir he sprayed can't mask the smell of our brisk walk because he's all worked up now.

"Don't you move," he orders in a hardened whisper. "And don't talk to any men, especially if they aren't holding a briefcase. They're the criminals."

I nod, hoping he'll go away soon because I've been holding my breath all this time, and I'm positive my face is turning blue.

Court has already started and once the judge sees the back of my father's head, it's as if he recognizes it and calls Bared Garrata's name next.

"Counselor," the judge begins. "I understand there's reason for you and your client to be in my courtroom again?"

"Yes, your honor. A very disturbing reason."

On the way to the defense attorney's table, my father stops to touch the shoulder of a woman with dark blond hair pulled back in a bun. Gratefully, she takes his hand, and I don't see how my father stands it, all that emotional pressure from defendants, from their loved ones, looking up to him as their only chance at being cleared of the charges levied against them by the entire State of California.

From a side door, a bald man in an orange jumpsuit appears. His beard is dark and bushy. He stands inside what looks like a jury box except there's no jurors, no chairs, and there's metal mesh screen separating him from the rest of the courtroom. Even at this distance, one of his eyes is visibly swollen and closed. A thick scab covers the bridge of his nose.

"Your Honor." My father levels his arm dramatically toward Bared, leveling his accusation. "Look at my client. He is an innocent man unless proven guilty. Bail must be reduced if he's to survive until his trial date. Who protected his rights last night while he was getting his face rammed against a steel sink, being called a sand nigger?"

"Enough, Counselor," admonishes the judge, raising his voice and lowering the gavel. "You will not play the race card in my courtroom."

My father nods, and something passes between them, the certainty that as a defense attorney it's my father's job to be a showman. To distract and offend. The judge looks a little familiar, and I think I've seen him once at a party at the home of my Uncle Dimitri—also a lawyer.

The prosecutor, a woman that's model tall, with short dark hair and pointy glasses, speaks up, forced to deal with my father's underhanded move.

"If Mr. Garrata surrenders his passports, I find nothing wrong with reducing his bail to three hundred thousand."

My father cocks his head.

"Three? How about one and a half." He points again at Bared. "This man has no priors. He's a family man with two young daughters. He's an assistant manager at a fan manufacturing plant." Now my father turns his attention on the prosecutor. "Ms. Tomkins needs to stop blowing hot air, so to speak. My client doesn't have that kind of collateral."

Some minor wrangling occurs before the judge ultimately rules in my father's favor, increasing the bail to one hundred and seventy-five to save face. And although I'm happy to see my father win, it feels like he's lost. Not only has his client, Bared Garrata, shot and killed someone pointblank, he must've blown a hole in the heart of every member of his victim's family.

Quickly, I turn and head out into the hall before I happen to recognize any of them by their grief.

* * *

That afternoon my mother comes home and three days later we are given my brother, all pink, with a clean bill of health, plus a birth certificate with his tiny footprint. Because my mother is still sore from the caesarean and because she wants to keep a closer eye on baby Nick, she has my father move my old mattress out of the garage and into Nick's room.

At least this is the story they tell me. I want to believe them, yet I can't help thinking about what Rhea said, how it sounded like he'd done something to hurt our mother. Whether out of necessity or penance, my father sets up my old bed in Nick's room. He screws in the last bolt of the bed frame, screwing himself, as he must've known, along with it. The nights he'd spend alone in the California King for months to come, maybe longer. Last spring for my birthday, my mother was insistent on buying me a waterbed. At the time I was blinded by having been given something so extravagant that I hadn't even asked for, that I had to actually fill up with a hose. But I see now she might've been planning on moving out of her own bedroom since then and the extra bed was no more of a gift to me than it was for herself.

* * *

Later in the night I hear them keeping their voices down, and this time it's my mother who speaks in the low roar.

"You at least could've told me what you did. I had to find out from the nurse. You had no plans of ever telling me."

"Jesus, June. I was only thinking of you."

"You were thinking of yourself."

"They already had you open. I didn't see the point in making you go through that again."

"It wasn't your fucking choice to make."

Rarely have I heard my mother use the F word and when she does, I know at least for her, the fight is over.

Uneasily, I close my eyes as if pretending that I already am might help me fall back asleep.

* * *

Within a week my family slips into a certain pattern of taking care of Nicholas—feedings, cradlings in the rocker, late night pacing up and down the hall. He seems to fall asleep to my off-key version of Duran Duran's ballad "Save a Prayer" so long as I don't spike my voice toward the high notes I can't reach. Diaper changes are round the clock, and I quickly learn the hard way, when changing him, to throw another diaper over his privates to stop the geyser that spurts on instinct as soon as I rip off the soiled one. Even my father pitches in when he gets home from work. All of us do except for Rhea.

Her pink window blinds stay clamped shut night and day. She sleeps for the rest of us who aren't getting much of it because of the baby, and with our mother in full nesting mode, Rhea has no reason to ever emerge from her own isolated nest she's created out of bed and blankets. If she's made any friends at her new school, like she claims, we've never met them. She even missed her last appointment with her shrink, using Nick's homecoming as an excuse. It seems she's even reduced her intake of Diet Coke just so she won't have to get up and use the bathroom.

One morning around my brother's third or fourth week home, my mother is in the kitchen fixing breakfast while my father is getting dressed for work. For once he doesn't have to bang on my sister's door. She's already showered and there is the muffled whirring of the blow dryer in the bathroom.

When she appears in the kitchen, she is dressed for school, her short hair finger-styled. The hot pink blouse she's wearing is new and matches her favorite Clinique lipstick. My mother's face brightens as she stands over the stove scrambling eggs, with my brother gurgling in his carrier on the floor, her bare foot tipping him contentedly back and forth. One less child she needs to worry about.

"You look pretty," my mother says. "I like the shirt. That's a flattering color against your fair skin."

The compliment makes Rhea's eyes shine and in those few seconds, I see them, really see them, before she retreats back into herself, into the morning routine of slinging her backpack over one shoulder and passing on breakfast.

"I'm glad you like it, Mom."

"Paula," my mother orders. "Give her a piece of your toast."

While I'm biting into a piece smothered in strawberry jam, I hold another one out to her, one that is only buttered, fewer calories. Rhea ignores it and leans down near my face. Instantly I raise my hands, expecting her to pinch or smack me like she usually does when she's in a good mood and wants to give me a hard time.

Instead, she kisses my cheek.

"What's the matter?" I ask, forgetting my mouth is full. "Are you on your period or something? You're acting weird."

Rhea laughs as she pulls away, a laugh that doesn't sound like it comes from her, no trademark snort that leaves the rest of us going in her wake.

* * *

After school I break out the bareback pad and the bridle and put them on Boo Boo. Going on Tomoko's advice, this is my prime opportunity to catch Cheech's attention.

He's outside swinging the bat at his own pop-ups, knocking the homers into the neighbor's backyard nursery on the other side. His father and little brother are nowhere in sight, probably at Rigo's Little League game.

Leading Boo Boo to the side of his corral, I climb up and keep him steady as I ease onto his back. The pad feels puffy and soft under my bare legs. If my mother were home she'd kill me, knowing I was riding this way, in nothing but a pair of shorts and my Vans. When she gives me lessons, I'm forced to wear jeans and riding boots, sometimes even gloves.

Right now, though, I've lucked out because she's not around. All I found after my father's secretary, Nora, dropped me off from school was a note she left on the fridge, instructing me to stay put and wait for my father. Nora wasn't much help either except she did stop off at McDonald's and buy me a Happy Meal before depositing me curbside.

The oleander bushes are abuzz, the hard shells of the flies reflecting in the sunlight, and I make sure and steer Boo Boo as far away as possible while still making a ring in our backyard of pure dirt. First I make kissing sounds, the cue for him to trot, keeping my back straight, squeezing with my thighs, so I won't slip around on the pad.

With each lap, I become more and more tense as I no longer hear Cheech swinging at anything. He's watching me, and I think twice if I should head back into the house and change into a pair of long pants. He's doing exactly what I wanted him to do, checking out the summer tan on my bare legs.

But there is no wave, no cat calling, not even a two-fingered whistle, and the rhythmic sound of bat connecting with ball resumes. Being ignored frustrates me into kicking it up a notch, and I touch Boo Boo's flank with my heel, feeling the slide and pull underneath me as his front legs extend into a gallop. I shorten my reins and somehow this accidentally brings Boo Boo too close to the oleander bushes. This is when I feel it land, as light as a barrette: a horse fly right on the side of my head.

Although I stop from screaming, I can't stop my hands from striking and slapping at my head like a lunatic. Maybe it is the commotion that startles my horse, or maybe it is the fact I drop the reins. In a matter of seconds Boo Boo lunges one way, and I slide off in another. The number one lesson my mother has drilled into my head is that if I'm going to fall, I need to drop, then roll away fast, so I won't get hoofed in the face.

I roll more smoothly and farther than perhaps a stunt double even could, stopping face down near the lower steps that lead up to the house. Dust is thick and powdery on my tongue, and I'm afraid to see if Cheech has just gotten a front row view of me eating dirt. Boo Boo grazes nearby, weeds poking out from the steel bit in his mouth, the seat of the bareback pad now hanging under his belly.

"Man, that's some wipeout," Cheech hollers from across the fences. "You okay?"

As I climb up to my knees, what feels like a relatively safe landing turns out to be anything but. I open my mouth to breathe, to answer Cheech, yet nothing comes in or out. The air is pounded from my lungs, and it seems with every gasp that they're clamping tighter and tighter. Breathing feels like an act I've never tried before, and I wonder if this is how Nicholas felt when he was first pulled out from the womb. I'm convinced that at age twelve, I'm dying of a heart attack.

Suddenly the back door opens and my father stands at the top of the stairs. From this angle, he strikes an imposing figure, blocking the sunlight.

"Paula, stop screwing around." My name explodes from his mouth in that same voice I've heard Moses use on his kids, his Vietnam voice. Though my father never served, it's as if he, too, is threatened and shell shocked by the sound of his own fear. Apparently me on all fours, all scuffed up on the ground doesn't seem to faze him. He comes down the steps. "Get up. We need to go. Your sister," he says. "She's tried to kill herself."

RIDE

There is no time for me to clean up and I'm forced to ride with my father to the hospital in a pair of denim shorts ripped at the side seam and a dirty navy blue T-shirt with white lettering that reads, *Jesus is a Greek*—a gift from my yia yia. In the car, my father briefly tells me what happened. Instead of raiding the fridge for food like most teens, this morning my sister raided the medicine cabinet of our bathroom, popping every pill out of its sealed packet or pour from its bottle—Benadryl, Tylenol, and the rest of her prescribed antidepressant, Prozac. Some she chewed so they'd take effect sooner while others she swallowed.

However, somewhere along the twenty-minute drive to LaVerne, she had a change of heart and before losing consciousness right there in first period Latin, she requested a pass to see the nurse. An ambulance was called and she was taken to the nearest hospital in Pomona where they forced liquid coal down her throat to dilute the drugs before inserting the tubes that would reach into her stomach and pump out the contents.

My face holds as hard as my father's, yet just below my right knee

I feel the blood like a tear from a fresh cut when I fell off Boo Boo. Quickly, I take off both of my socks, curl up in the passenger seat, and press one against my shin.

The ride to the hospital is long, practically a hundred miles away in Long Beach and my father talks nearly non-stop, detailing his plans for Rhea.

"We need to get your sister involved in something."

"I think it's a little too late for a hobby."

"Of course it isn't. She needs something to distract her from herself. This is all about boredom."

If my mother were riding shotgun, she'd fire off at the mouth at him, and she'd be right. What he's saying doesn't make any sense. Still, I'm curious to hear what he has in mind.

"What exactly?"

"Horses."

"We already have two in the backyard."

"No," my father says. He lets up on the gas as if he must slow the car down in order to better explain things to me.

Behind us a pick-up honks and swerves into the fast lane to avoid hitting our bumper. Normally my father would react. Even if it was his fault, he'd still curse the driver out in Greek. He'd motion for the guy to pull over. "You've got to get the *minara* to take the first punch," my father would say. "Then you beat him good and it still appears like self-defense." In all my life no driver has ever taken my father up on the challenge. When anybody gets that close to him, it must become all too clear that he truly is one mad Greek.

Shockingly, this time my father blocks out the road rage, impassive to the other driver, riding next to us, his face made ugly by anger.

"I mean show horses," my father continues as if our conversation was never interrupted. "The kind you earn blue ribbons on. I have a new client who owns a restaurant by the airport. His daughter trains Walking Horses."

"Walking Horses," I repeat, a little confused. "Isn't that what all horses do? Walk?"

My father speeds up, visibly irritated, and I fear he might be having second thoughts about catching up with that driver of the pick-up.

"It's a breed. They're popular in the South. From what I hear, they're a goddamn goldmine."

Buying my sister this type of a horse doesn't sound like a cure-all, yet having thought of it, my father appears relieved, at least for now, of some of the pain of knowing his oldest daughter has just tried to end her life.

By the time we reach Long Beach Memorial, he decides to drive right past and onto Ocean Boulevard, where we stop at Tower Records.

"What are we doing here?"

"I want to get your sister something."

It seems dead wrong buying someone a gift who just botched a suicide attempt—a kind of reward for having second thoughts? But I guess he doesn't want to show up empty-handed.

Before he gets out, he looks at me hard, for potential cracks, for ways into reading my face, like I imagine he does witnesses on the stand right before he tears into their testimony.

"She doesn't have a boyfriend?"

I keep my eyes level, feeling like a liar even though I'm telling the truth.

"Not that I know of."

"She didn't tell you anything?"

"No, Dad," I say, opening my door. "Rhea doesn't exactly like me. Ask Mom. She usually tells her everything."

Dissatisfied with my answer, my father gets out of the car and walks ahead of me.

I re-snap the barrettes holding the sides of my hair back and slap the dust off my shirt. Impatient, but trying not to show it, my father waits at the entrance, waving a hand toward the wall of cassette tapes.

"Pick out a couple for her."

Immediately I head over to the New Wave section and grab The Cure's *Japanese Whispers* and nearly get her INXS, before settling on Wham!'s latest, *Make it Big,* in the hopes she'll let me record a copy of it later.

It still hasn't sunk in that my sister tried to take her own life, that she stopped wanting to share it with me, with Nicholas, with our mother and father. We'd all watched her withdraw and sleep. Countless times one of us would knock on her door, attempting to coax her out. In a sense, she'd been dying inside for months, starving her body, entombing it in her room as if she were already dead.

None of us knew how to stop her, not even the L.A. shrink. Only Rhea is able to judge how much pain she can endure. At some point, after she woke up this morning, while standing before the open medicine cabinet, she must've closed down inside. In all those pill bottles, less than an arm's length away, were the means of reaching terminal relief.

The gift my father has in mind is a giant boom box. He comes at me with it, holding it the wrong way, by the handle at his side. They're also known as ghetto blasters, the bigger the better, and are supposed to rest heavy on one shoulder, while you walk everywhere, blaring music.

I'm surprised it even has a handle. This one is a Sanyo beauty with dual stereos and tape decks, with a cord, and it also takes double D batteries.

He motions at me from line and on my way over I switch out Wham! for INXS.

"What did you get her?" he asks.

I drop the cassettes in their awkward plastic anti-theft packaging on the counter.

"INXS and The Cure."

My father shakes his head as he hands over his credit card to the cashier, a young guy in his late teens with spiky punk hair and a silver stud in his bottom lip.

"The excess cure? You'd better watch that smart ass mouth of yours."

The cashier smiles a little as he punches in the numbers of my father's credit card.

"I didn't mean anything, Dad," I say in my defense. "They're just her two favorite bands."

From the inside pocket of my shorts, I cross my fingers. I wish he were paying with cash. It's always a crapshoot whether my father's credit card will go through. We've been humiliated at the finest restaurants in town — Benihana, The Velvet Turtle, even once in line at Kmart. I don't see how Tower Records will be any different.

My father keeps track of paying bills the way he balances his checkbook, which is rarely. Having somebody ask for another form of payment never stops him from spending money he doesn't have. He just reaches in his wallet for another piece of plastic. This time when the cashier frowns at the register, I make my break for it, slipping out through the electric doors.

* * *

Rhea is under a seventy-two hour lockdown at the psychiatric unit in Long Beach Memorial Hospital. Why she was taken so far away from Chino, I'm not sure. My father says it was my mother's idea. Of course I'm too young to see her.

As consolation my father promises he'll tell her I picked out the music for her new ghetto blaster.

From the parking lot, I can't see the ocean. But it's close enough to smell the salty tang of the water, mixed with the car exhaust, and I'm reminded of someplace better. I'm reminded of my favorite water ride, the Log Ride, at Knott's Berry Farm with Rhea, both of us sharing the same log, holding up our arms, braving the steep drop.

In the lobby Yia Yia sits with Nicholas sleeping in his carrier on the cushion beside her. My father must've called her to drive over from nearby Lakewood and watch the baby. I doubt if she came alone. Even though Uncle Gil is pushing forty, he rarely leaves her side.

When Uncle Gil sees us, he taps the glass hard with his pinky ring, letting us, especially my father, know he's outside on the patio smoking his pipe. With his bouts of rage, with his creepy interest in my family instead of his own, and his inability to get along with anybody other than his mother, he makes me think he belongs in a psychiatric unit more than a teenage girl who got a little depressed and swallowed some Tylenol. Through the thick and darkened glass, he's already spotted the rip in my shorts. Sometimes he looks at my mother in the exact way when he comes over for dinner. All I know at my age then is that it's a wrong look because it's coming from a relative. Today, as a thirty-eight-year-old woman, I know that that expression suggests something far more than sexual attraction. Behind it is a private sexual want that demeans and isolates, making me feel unsafe. Instinctively, defensively, I look out for it in the eyes of all men from the strangers I come across on the street to colleagues at my work and even my husband's friends. Because of Uncle Gil, my guard is never down.

But back in that dreary hospital lobby his weird focus on me registers as just a bad feeling and I shiver and pull on my father's coat sleeve.

"Dad," I lie. "I'm cold."

My father takes off his sports jacket and drapes it over my shoulders. The weight of his hand on me feels reassuring, like things are finally under his control. His greeting with Yia Yia is short, which never seems to bother her. In fact, she seems to prefer it that way. I've never seen her hug any of her children.

Her affection is reserved for her grandkids, as if she must be one step removed from her offspring in order to show any.

Her hair, dyed black and shaped in fashionable old lady helmet style, is dented in the back as if she'd been lying down when she got the call. She's wearing one navy blue open-toed sandal and one black. What has just happened with my sister is probably furrowing new ground on Yia Yia's face, and I try not to stare at her wrinkles.

She doesn't say much except to point me in the direction of the restroom where I can wash up.

When I return, she tells me not to worry.

"You know this crazy part is coming from your mother's side," Yia Yia explains to me. "Your mother's father was a barstool drunk. Unfortunately for your sister, she's taken after that side. She'll always be weak."

She grabs my chin and scrutinizes my face. Her fingers are tough from working with steel parts at a factory that manufactures automobile thermostats for the second half of her life, after my pappou died. The first half, she took in the neighbor's ironing to help put her three boys through college.

I try to hold still. I try not to show how much she's hurting me.

"Nobody has to worry about you, Paula," she says. "You're a Priamos. You look like one. And you're strong like one too."

Whether Yia Yia's blessing me or damning me, I can't decide. Only after my eyes tear up does she finally let go.

Later, as my parents come off the elevator, I notice my father fall behind my mother. The boom box is gone, and he's talking with a man in a white coat, a doctor. The man appears flattered as he takes my father's card and shakes his hand.

"I'm looking forward to meeting with him," the man says. He's younger than my father by a few years.

They're doing business. My father must've seen an opportunity to ask this doctor, no doubt my sister's doctor, to be an expert witness in Bared's upcoming trial. I'd overheard my father talking to Bared's wife after the court hearing. He was looking for a psychiatrist from a respectable hospital.

My father has killed two birds with one stone, and I can see my mother must be thinking this same thing because it looks as if she'd like to hurl a rock straight at his head. And even though this is just a fleeting look she gives him, a look he doesn't even catch, their marriage has suffered yet another blow.

WHAT THEY TOLD ME AFTER HE DIED

Yeah, I think I saw him in here before. He'd come in around seven, stay 'til closing. Tipped big even though he only drank straight Coke. Swear to God. Not sure how anybody can stay sober in a joint like this. Maybe he slipped his own brand of choice in here. Would make more sense, I guess. I'm kind of surprised, though. I didn't think he had a daughter. He seemed like a lonely guy with no family.

—Greg Douglas, bartender at the Kat Nip

I know he's your father and all, but facts are facts. The son of a bitch had it coming.

—Rex O'Dell, former client and business partner

You have it wrong. He had no plans of moving out. Those boxes were there because he was trying to move more of his stuff into storage. That's a small room, you know.

—Yia Yia

Never seen him before. You're sure you have the right place?

—Nigel Watkins, owner of the Kat Nip

There will be no obituary. It's bad enough word might leak out before he's in the ground.

—Uncle Dimitri

I took nothing from that man. He was the fucking thief. Aren't most lawyers?

—Rex O'Dell

You best stop duckin' my calls, motherfucker. Or I'll come see you personally.

—Unidentified man, left on the voice mail of my father's cell phone

I could've gone to dead. Your father, he saved me. May God rest his soul.

—Bared Garratta, former client

How do you think I feel? My husband's gone and none of you will even let me come out there to show my respects. Nobody will let me bury him once and for all.

—June Priamos, ex-wife

Why do you keep going back to Gil? Yes, he should've done things differently that morning. Don't make this about what he did to you.

—Uncle Dimitri

SAY UNCLE

My sister's new hobby is partly responsible for why I'm seated Indian style in front of the TV watching *The Young and the Restless* as Uncle Gil kneels behind me and hikes up the back of my T-shirt. He's so close I can feel the palm-sized handgun he keeps in the front pocket of his seventies style OP corduroy shorts. His hands are wet with baby oil. I hear the slapping and sucking sounds they make when he rubs them together.

My arm reaches behind me because I am afraid to look.

"I don't want a massage. My back isn't sore."

"Nonsense," he says. "That was a long plane ride. Your splenius muscles are tight."

He is no expert on the human body. He is a failed inventor who prides himself on knowing things others have no time to learn. He uses this knowledge at family get-togethers so that he doesn't appear idle, so it doesn't look like he's leeching off his mother, my Yia Yia's Social Security checks. He's lived with Yia Yia ever since leaving his wife over a decade earlier while she was seven months pregnant. In Yia Yia's garage, he stores Liqui-Steal, his latest invention, a spray on substance that hardens into something like metal and repels rust. With no ordinary amount of caution, he empties out those oxygen-tanks-on-wheels commonly used for the elderly and fills them with Liqui-Steal. He must do this, he says, to throw the powerful steel lobbyists off his scent.

Uncle Gil and I are alone in the house, my house in Chino. He's babysitting me for the rest of the Memorial Day weekend while my family stays in Tennessee for a horse show my sister is riding in, her first one out of state. In less than six months, my father has bought two horses—one for Rhea, a palomino gelding, "his goldmine," named Good As Gold. The other horse, Pride's Contract, is a black stallion he purchased for himself.

Like a real horse trader, in exchange for the fifty grand price tag, my father has shelled out twenty-five thousand in cash and offered his legal services free of charge for the next twenty-four months to Gold's former owners who own the Fly Bye Café near the Ontario airport. He's defending the couple in a frivolous lawsuit brought on by a customer who claims she suffered second-degree burns from a scalding hot wiener that slipped out of the bun and disfigured her chin. The woman is asking for two hundred thousand for medical bills, lost wages, and mental pain and anguish. After all, she now has to dab concealer on the reddish nickel-sized spot on her skin left behind by the runaway hot dog.

The high-priced stallion is supposedly paid for with the hefty retainer Bared had ponied up. Defending a homicide charge doesn't come cheap even if a plea bargain is reached and it never goes to trial. With the expert witness from Long Beach Memorial waiting in the wings to back up Bared's claim of temporary insanity, the Prosecutor settles on a ten-year sentence at a maximum security psychiatric facility. And with good, meaning sound, behavior, Bared will be out in five years before his daughters are my age and enter middle school.

Uncle Gil turns down the TV and it's in my uncertainty about his real motives, in those brief seconds while I decide how to get out of this, that he makes his move. His warm hands slipping all over my skin worries me. I know things could get far worse.

He has never tried getting this close to me before except once when I was five or six. One night after dinner at Yia Yia's house, as the family sat around the table of dirty dishes, Uncle Gil got up out of his chair and came over to mine, squatting on his haunches. In the late seventies, he drove a yellow Datsun hatchback called the "honeybee model" with a customized black swirl along the side doors and a happy bee with its stinger in a honey jar. Buzzing at me was his joke that I didn't find at all funny. "Buzzy, buzzy bee," he said, cramming his face in mine. Uncle Gil wore glasses, and I imagined knocking them right off his face. "Stop it," I warned. "Or I'll punch you."

"Buzzy, buzzy bee." Maybe it was the way he laughed after he said it again or maybe it was my parents' refusal to take my threat seriously. So to prove I meant business, I landed one dead center, right on the bridge of his nose, the lenses going cock-eyed. Uncle Gil lurched back so quickly that the soles of his rubber slippers slid out from underneath him and he landed ass-first on the kitchen linoleum. Yia Yia had mopped it to a shine right before we came over. "Paul," Uncle Gil shouted at my father from the floor, "aren't you going to do something?" But my hitting his brother struck my father as hysterical, the choking, coughing kind that took a napkin for his eyes and a sip of water to recover from. "Stop being such a *mounee*, Gil. She said she was sick of you impersonating a goddamn bee."

During the commercial break when I'm about to get up, Uncle

Gil's hands hold me down, pressing harder and harder on my shoulders. His fingers fumble and tug at the hook in the back of my bra to work it loose, and I cross my arms, an impenetrable barrier, so he won't sneak his way around to my chest.

The slider is a few feet away, but from where I'm sitting it may as well be a mile. I see no way out.

He fingers the muscles in my neck, and I lunge forward.

"I told you," he says, mistaking my reflex for physical pain. "You're too young to be this tense."

Every sound is louder than it should be. The air conditioner. His heavy breathing, the catch in it when his hands run freely under my curly hair, then down the length of my spine.

On screen, a woman with long blonde hair orders a bell-hop to set up portable fans around her. The a/c in her hotel suite has broken down. She gathers her hair on top of her head and kneels before the whirling blades.

Uncle Gil's breath reeks of vitamins and his skin of Coppertone even though he's spent the entire day inside the house.

"Now she's a pretty one," he says. "Don't you think she's pretty?"

At thirteen I'm old enough to see what he's trying to do, how he's trying to turn a soap opera into some kind of porno. I squirm out of his reach and make for the slider.

Once outside, I take what seems like my first real breath since this morning when my mother sprung it on me that I was leaving early on a flight with Uncle Gil. She held off until the last minute because she knew I'd protest.

I don't know if he'll come after me. In this open air, though, the odds seem better.

The smog is heaviest in late afternoon, clouding the bare slopes of Mt. Baldy in a pink blur. I decide to wait things out, for however long it takes, on the diving board until the air clears. Pierre, my toy poodle with chunky curls, jumps at my back, and I scoop him up and hold him against my chest. My toes dangle high above the water.

Before we moved here, we sat around the dinner table as a family, and designed the pool from scratch. The long steps that plaster the length of it were my mother's idea.

The brown tile with blue swirls was my sister's. My father and I came up with how deep the end would be—nine feet—perfect for testing out our lung capacity by diving for shiny quarters or rubber rings from its floor.

Sometimes my father tosses bigger money, silver dollars, the kind he wins in casinos and saves in a jar from our trips to Lake Tahoe. While I'm greedily retrieving them, he'll span the entire length of the pool, back and forth, bottom feeding like a giant stingray. It's the closest we ever get to swimming together.

The Murrillo brothers are loud next door, splashing around blindly in their pool.

"Marco!" Rigo hollers.

"Polo!" shouts Cheech.

The pool is the only place in the backyard where the Murrillos can't see me. Blocking their view is the eyesore gazebo one of my father's druggie clients named Bud constructed earlier this year to work off his legal fees. He's a carpenter from Venice Beach who moonlights as an artist. His creative side shows a little too much in the details. The posts are made from old telephone poles and the latticework is eclectic strips of red wood, pine, and birch, any wood Bud could find in the scrap pile at the lumber yard. Before he could shake up the spray paint, my father assured him it was a job well done.

Something makes me look toward the house. Uncle Gil must've been watching all this time because the family room curtains move before falling back into place.

* * *

Right after dinner that night, Uncle Gil bolts out of his chair, knocking it over. In his excitement, he doesn't bother to right it. A bucket of Kentucky Fried Chicken and Styrofoam containers of mashed potatoes and coleslaw are on the table. Nothing is left on his plate but a couple of clean bones and a soggy yellow bag with a half-eaten ear of corn sticking out.

He karate chops the air with his hands, and I glimpse the bulletproof vest he wears under his Hawaiian print shirt.

"You need to learn some self-defense moves."

Along with the bulletproof vest he ordered from a survivalist catalog, he also owns the U.S. Marine Corp's *Close Combat*, the U.S. Army's *Hand-to-Hand Fighting*, and another one with a dragon on the cover for the Special Forces. Behind the door to his bedroom, several rifles hang by their leather holsters. I've seen him slice open his mail with a razor sharp knife that's encased like a ballpoint pen. He keeps mace like others do hairspray in the medicine cabinets of every bathroom in Yia Yia's house.

Now Uncle Gil shuffles around in rubber sandals, punching the air like a boxer. Suddenly, he stops and spreads his legs, then reaches out to me. He flattens his palms and curls his fingers, and I recognize the stance from the cover of one of his combat fighter books.

"Go ahead and grab my penis."

What he says doesn't make sense. There can't be moves like that in his handbooks. I'm getting a sick feeling that what happened this afternoon was just a preview of what is to come, and I fear how the rest of this night alone with him, acting this way, will play out. My parents won't be home for another fifteen and a half hours.

With my plate still full, I use a cold chicken breast and runny baked beans as my excuse. I poke at a few with my fork.

"I'm not finished eating."

His dark eyes are mere slits and perspiration bubbles up in the temples of his graying Brillo hair from all that jibing and ducking. He's nowhere near defeated.

"You need to smarten up. There are bad guys out there who want to hurt pretty young girls like you."

Pierre scratches at the glass. Usually by this time, I let him in, but I can't. When Uncle Gil was a kid, Yia Yia had to give away a black lab named Inky because she caught Gil holding its paws under scalding hot water, a punishment for digging in the backyard.

I ignore him and get up from the table and rinse my dish in the kitchen sink.

Uncle Gil is close behind. Before I have time to put the plate in the dish washer, he yanks it from my hands and tosses it on the linoleum, breaking it Greek style, as if what is happening now is somehow cause for celebration.

"Go on," he says. In his frustration, he takes a couple steps back, then forward again. He can't keep still. He can't keep his hand off the gun in his front pocket. "Grab my penis, Paula. C'mon, give me your best shot. Don't make me make you."

A portrait of my father's prized new stallion hangs behind Uncle Gil on the wall. Valued at over a quarter of a million, the horse is captured in the throes of winning first place, a blue ribbon flowing from its bridle, its former owner on top. She's an attractive blond and looks like she picks up her children from school in one of those BMW station wagons.

I don't understand why my mother isn't jealous, my father having blown up a picture of this woman and nailed it in the center of our dining room. She laughed when I asked her about it. "It isn't the woman I'm worried about," she'd said. "It's your father's ego. He won't be satisfied until he buys up the best and sells nothing. He'll bankrupt us."

My strength doesn't come from hating that picture. It doesn't come from hating how my father earned the money. It comes from hating the position Uncle Gil keeps placing me in. It comes from hating him.

I don't need a combat book to know the strongest part of my body is my head, and I use it to ram his chest.

The bullet proof vest absorbs the brunt of it, but he does lose his balance and stumbles back against the wall, cracking the glass in the picture frame with his elbow.

It's not the loaded handgun he could pull out at any second, but the sound of our struggle that sets me to flight. The safest place I can think of is my parents' room, where I lock the door. From their slider, I let in Pierre, then snap that secured too. I take him and the phone from the nightstand into the bathroom.

First I try my best friend Tomo. Her mother answers and I hear Japanese in the background on her TV. "She's at volleyball practice, Paula." She sounds strangely reluctant, almost friendly, and I wonder if she's catching on yet. The season doesn't start for another month.

Volleyball practice is just a cover for Tomo to see her boyfriend, Jesse. "I'll tell my Tomo-chan you called," her mother says.

After I set down Pierre, I straddle the edge of the tub and call the hotel where my family is staying. I have the number written on the inside of my forearm so I won't forget. Pierre trots around, barking at the commotion. Outside the window is a small garden, enclosed from the rest of the yard with a high wooden fence. My mother grows tomatoes, carrots and bell peppers. She likes to open the window while soaking in the tub and smell fresh vegetables. It makes her feel as if she's living in the country.

My fingers are shaky, and I must've punched the wrong number because an old man with a lazy drawl answers. "Sorry," I say, in case I've waked him, then I hang up and re-dial.

This time, I reach my mother.

She sounds out of breath, or out of patience. I can't decide which.

"Your sister placed second. I think she looked great out there. Your father, of course, thinks she was robbed."

"Tell her I said congratulations." Truth is, at this moment, I couldn't care less what color ribbon my sister has won. I raise my voice to talk over Pierre who's still barking. "Uncle Gil is acting weird."

My mother sighs loud into the phone.

"Of course he's acting weird. He is weird. That doesn't mean you shouldn't listen to him."

"He rubbed my back," I said. "Even when I told him not to."

For a moment, my mother listens. "Paula," she starts. "Maybe you're seeing too much into it because you don't like him. We'll be home by the time you get out of school tomorrow. If he's made you uncomfortable, just tell him you're tired and go to bed early."

Before I have the chance to get to what just happened, she tells me she loves me, then hangs up.

One of the stakes that holds up the tomato vines in my mother's garden snaps.

Pierre growls.

Then there's tapping on the window, and part of me knows without looking he's found another way in.

His hairy big toes are what I see first, planted firmly in the garden. He smiles in that same honeybee way.

"Didn't I tell you, Paula? Look how easy it would be for somebody to break through this glass."

In bed that night I don't sleep. All three of the phones in the house are with me. Mine is plugged in the wall jack. I can be the only one who calls in or out. Even with this line of defense, I lay awake, Pierre safely under the covers and my desk chair angled beneath the doorknob. From underneath the door I watch him hesitate on the other side, blocking out the light in the hallway. I know why he's standing there. Uncle Gil is running out of time to get me to touch his penis.

Before the door knob turns, before he does something crazier than he's already done like blast a hole right through the door, I think fast. I think of how much he thinks of my father, and I pray that'll be enough to stop him at least for tonight.

"Goodnight, Uncle Gil," I call out. "I just got off the phone with my dad. He said to stop acting like a *mounee* and let me get some sleep."

"Does he want me to call him back?"

"No," I shout, petrified my plan might backfire.

"It's even later back there. They're two hours ahead, remember?"

When my parents return I see no point in telling them about

Uncle Gil showing up in my mother's garden.

They're home now and my mother promises me she'll never allow him to babysit me again. "I shouldn't have let him in the first place," she says. "I just didn't want you missing another day of school."

For the next couple weeks Uncle Gil prepares for and heads to North Dakota where a farmer has flown him out to test coat the underbelly of one of his best John Deere tractors. He videotapes the spraying of the tractor piece by piece and mails my father the VHS tape. However, for reasons that remain top secret, Uncle Gil doesn't return with an order to spray the farmer's entire fleet.

"Somebody got to him," he explains to my father at dinner his first night back.

We live ten minutes from the Ontario airport and it's no coincidence why Uncle Gil chooses to book his return flight there instead of LAX, which is much closer to Yia Yia's house. Piling it on thick for my father's benefit comes first before unpacking any suitcase. "All it takes is one phone call," he continues. "Those Midwestern boys are paid off by the government not to grow crops. They suck off the taxpayers more than single mothers on welfare."

This part doesn't sound right, considering he left his own wife no other choice but to become a single mother before she ever gave birth to my cousin Althea. Every other weekend Althea used to come over and we'd play outside, salting the slugs that squirmed and ate their way through Yia Yia's garden, watching them foam up and die. Or on the days we didn't feel like doing Yia Yia's dirty work, we'd search for clues and trace each other's Big Foot imprints made from our Buster Brown shoes between the rows of cabbage and tomatoes. On one Friday afternoon, the day Althea was supposed to be dropped off, a letter showed up in the mail in her place. In Althea's first grade scrawl, she told her father she wanted nothing more to do with him. At dinner that night Uncle Gil showed all of us the letter. "I hate you," it read. "You're NOT my daddy anymore." Instead of taking Althea's mother to court like most fathers in the same situation, Uncle Gil did something scary. He bought a plot and marker for his daughter at a local cemetery using the date the letter was postmarked as the day Althea died.

Whether my father buys Uncle Gil's theory about the farmer or pities him is no matter. Uncle Gil is the youngest, the weakest member in a generation of brothers that were raised for the unspoken purpose of providing Yia Yia with bragging rights over their successes with her two sisters at Sunday brunch after worship. As a sign of encouragement, my father offers up the extra room in his law office rent free.

At that news I quickly excuse myself from the table. Even my mother's lasagna can't keep me here. She bakes it especially for me and goes light on the ricotta.

On my way into the kitchen, she comes up from behind with my plate. "Finish eating in your room," she whispers so that only I hear.

* * *

One day after Uncle Gil moves into the office, my sister comes home unexpectedly during her lunch break. Most of the time she picks up a taco salad from Boca Grande down the street from the office. I'm on summer vacation and she's no longer even getting an education. After the suicide attempt, my parents pulled her out of the Christian school. Rhea says the God part only made things worse because she believes that he somehow damned her in the mind. To fill up her days, when not at the stables in Ontario riding her horse, she works at my father's office, filing papers.

That afternoon she catches me out in the pool, kicking around in an inner tube. I'm not supposed to be in the water when nobody is home because my parents are afraid I could get a cramp and drown.

"Mom went grocery shopping," I say. "What do you want?" In order for her to stay silent, I'm expecting I'll have to do extra chores for her like feed the horses.

My sister says nothing. It's as if she doesn't even hear me. She is dressed in long flowing white pants, a bright v-necked blouse and spiked heels. Her hair is stylishly wrapped in a scarf she twists like a half turban, with only her bangs showing.

She and I are polar opposites in the looks department.

Without the traits of a typical Greek, she is attractive in a different way. Although she spends hours primping before the mirror, she never sees it and puts on too much make-up to draw out features that are better left alone. Whereas my eyes are big and brown and boring, hers are smaller and hazel, the kind that react in either gold or greens to the light that refracts in them. Her hair isn't the right texture to wear beyond the shoulders. Mine is halfway down my back and curly and my mother often yells at me to shampoo out the chlorine from the pool.

My sister sits down on a lounge chair, not realizing she's on my wet towel.

"They should've listened when you called that night."

I nod. My mother told her everything. The two of them keep no secrets from each other. Even my father gets jealous of their relationship.

My sister tells me how Uncle Gil came up behind her earlier

while she was straightening the papers and files on my father's desk. My father was in trial and his secretary, Nora, had called in sick.

Uncle Gil began rubbing her shoulders over her clothing. Quickly then, maybe in fear of being stopped, he reached around, then down her neckline, her bare breast held in his hand.

"Your bra is too tight," he explained. "You need something with a firm underwire. Would you like me to buy a pretty lace one for you?"

Too confused to question why her uncle was feeling her up, she chose not to answer him.

"I just sat there," she says.

The air is desert hot and the foundation she uses to even out her skin tone melts in splotches on her face. She has fallen apart in front of me in a way I've never seen before. When she tried to kill herself, she'd looked her very best. If she were to get up now, the seat of her pants would be soaked from the towel. Pierre comes up and licks her ankle and she stomps her heel to scare him off.

I never ask how long it went on with Uncle Gil. It isn't my place to judge. He is armed at all times with, at the very least, a small handgun and one knife. I do know it came right after he suggested he retrieve a beach towel and a bottle of baby oil from the trunk of his car. He wanted her to lie down and remove her panties so he could show her the technique he learned to relieve a woman's cramps. While he went out the back door and popped his trunk, she grabbed her car keys and fled through the front.

* * *

After my sister talks to our parents they finally react the right way, the way I imagined they would the night I first called my mother. With two daughters telling similar stories, Uncle Gil's twisted attention toward the two of us is something they can no longer ignore.

As my mother puts my baby brother down for the night, my father fires up his old pick-up, the one he uses to carry hay bales, and heads to his office where he loads the back with Uncle Gil's desk and file cabinets and oxygen tanks filled with Liqui-Steal. Then he drives back to the house and picks up my mother. Together they ride the hour that it takes to get to Yia Yia's house and later I will hear how my father provides door-to-door service, dumping everything on the front lawn. Even with the arsenal in his bedroom, Uncle Gil must've known better than to come out of the house while his older brother unloaded. He must've realized my father was packing a far more dangerous kind of heat. Initially my father did nothing, and it's this self-condemnation for not acting sooner, for not acting like a parent, that moves him to lift the kind of heavy things that are normally too much for even two men half his age.

Past midnight, while our parents are still gone, I drag my sleeping bag and pillow into my sister's bedroom. For once she and I have banded together against our parents and in our strength we've succeeded in getting Uncle Gil out of our lives, for what I hope will be for good. But what she and I share will be short lived because the fact is I fought him off quicker than she did and in a situation like molestation minutes and seconds count most. Because she feels she let it happen longer, she will ultimately view herself as more of a victim than a fighter. Sometimes I wonder if this experience hasn't permanently altered her self-esteem. The damage he caused might very well have resulted in making her more susceptible to the kind of men who would later come into her life.

Inside my sister's room that night it's dark and hard to see except for the mountainous outline of her on the mattress. In place of pajamas she's taken to wearing a pink terrycloth bathrobe to bed. Always so concerned with her weight, she wouldn't want to know how she reminds me of the slumbering Star Wars monster Jabba the Hut. She's breathing heavily in a deep, possibly medicated sleep, so I'm careful not to run into anything. If I do she might wake up grumpy and kick me out. She won't understand how badly I need to be in here with her. It isn't that I'm scared. There is no longer any reason to be. I'm just having trouble sleeping. On the floor beside my sister's bed, I zip up inside the bag and slow my breathing until it finally matches hers.

WHITE ELEPHANT

On the eve before that fateful trip when my father starts blowing large sums of his clients' money, I am spending what time I have left out on the front porch with Cheech. He leans in with his vanilla shake breath, about to kiss me for the first time when the porch light comes on, freezing him in his tracks. For two summers in a row, thanks to the Walking Horse show season, I've lost the chance to stand here, to experience the heat of his kiss. And now my father is forcing me to wait some more. The glare isn't bad enough. He has to open the front door and scowl.

"Holy fuck," Cheech whispers. He rips his hands so quick from my hips I have to take a step back to regain my balance.

The sight of my father, still wearing his suit pants and socks as if he doesn't want to leave behind telling footprints, is cause for some fast praying, as he looks more like a hired thug caught cleaning up after his murderous act than a defense lawyer. What looks like blood spatter on his white undershirt is actually marinara sauce. How he heard us drive up, I'm not sure. On my advice, Cheech killed the engine and coasted right after the stop sign.

Even a quick trip through a McDonald's drive-thru counts as a date in my father's eyes and here he stands, interrupting the best part.

I squint up at him, about to explain. The sound of Cheech's Pumas sprinting down the brick steps stop me. He's already halfway home, forgetting all about his blue Civic with the black hood sitting in front of my house. He's a year older than me and has just gotten his driver's license. This is why he came over to begin with, to brag and ask if I wanted a ride. Since he was thirteen, he worked potting trees, lugging bags of top soil next door at the neighbor's nursery, saving up for his first car. Later tonight when the coast is clear, he'll sneak over to retrieve it—or possibly tomorrow after we've left for Tennessee.

It's the beginning of July and the middle of the Walking Horse show season. My father is coming off another big win, this time getting the most popular member of our church, a Greek god with no steady girlfriend who owns a small liquor store Booze-O-Ouzo, found not guilty of rape. "A jury of mostly middle-aged housewives, no less," I hear my father boast over the phone to a friend. "The *papara* prosecutor thought he had it locked. But everybody knows older women turn on a younger one, especially when a man they wouldn't mind bedding down with is involved."

My mother, sister, and brother have already been back in the shallows of the South all month in a rental home. I've held out for as long as I can. My father will be staying for just a few days, while I'm being dragged kicking and screaming into a never-ending episode of that old country show *Hee Haw*, which will last until Labor Day.

I want to tell my father I'm innocent. Sure, I planned on kissing Cheech, but I wasn't certain if I'd even open my mouth. Behind the peephole, in the dark, my father must've imagined something far worse than a potential French kiss. Now that Cheech has fled the scene my father seems like he could care less. Mission accomplished, he shuts the door on me. Any other father might've said something, but not mine. This is the beginning of a silence that'll last all night over six states until the wheels of the 747 finally touchdown in Nashville.

*   *   *

Our seats are in first class instead of coach. At the risk of my father flying into a rage, I decide not to ask why we're seated up here, merely grateful for the extra room between us. The seats are bigger, I have my own armrest, and after breakfast the flight attendant comes by with a silver tong and a basket of hand cloths, warm and lemon-scented. Yet I'm unable to outright enjoy these luxuries because my father is not speaking to me. Close-mouthed punishment is far more relentless than a yelling fit, and I don't deserve either one. It was just a kiss. Cheech kept his hands respectfully at my hips.

Things with Tomo and her Latin boyfriend are much more intense. He's older, already out of high school, and tells her he loves her so she'll do the kind of below the belt acts that prove it. He drives a 1975 classic BMW, the sunroof always open, the chrome always too shiny. He picks her up after school, waiting for her on the east side of campus, the quiet side, near the English classrooms, the same place where I've designated my mother to pick me up so I won't be seen.

What hurts the most is that my father assumes I'm just like her and he's ashamed.

Determined to strike back, I do.

"Nothing happened last night, Dad." I place my headphones on my head, thumbing up the sound. "Your brother is the sick pervert."

What I say hits low and deep. This is my intention, of course, and the wreckage in my father's eyes makes me instantly want to take it back, to repair the damage I've just caused. None of us ever talk about what happened.

Rhea probably does, though that's in private session with her shrink. Since I fought off Psycho Gil, I must be okay. And I am. There's nothing wrong with me, and, in my family, not having to be on mood altering meds and getting good grades are the only ways to get yourself ignored.

* * *

My mother picks us up from the airport. She's alone in an Astro Van and after more than half an hour on a two-lane interstate, she turns off on a one-way road. She can't miss the exit because there stands a painted blue billboard with a Walking Horse in black silhouette, one of its front legs reaching out like an arrow toward more road.

We pass Bubba's Boot Barn, a store made of tin with giant tractor tires holding down the roof. Erected roadside is a sign with removable lettering that reads—*Ya'll flock to Bubba's! Ostrich leather on sale. Thirty percent off!* Next to Bubba's is a fireworks store that advertises in graffiti type red lettering across the front windows that it's open year round. Out front is a gleaming line of shopping carts.

I lean in between my parents. My father is busy studying the program of young horses that will be up for auction tomorrow at a stable called Lytle Creek Farms.

"Why would anybody set off fireworks other than the Fourth?" I ask.

"They're legal here twelve months out of the year, honey," my mother informs me, as if she's become an expert on the region in under a month. "It's part of their culture."

My father glances up from the program at the Bubba's sign.

"Remind me, Paula Girl. Before we leave, I'll pick you up some boots. You can stomp around like a cowgirl on the front porch for *Viva Zapata*."

That phrase must be the only Spanish my father knows.

Picking on Cheech's ethnicity is a new low even for a defense attorney because Cheech is no loser. He's a star athlete who attends private school. Many years later after my father has passed I'll come across that phrase again while in the classics section at Blockbuster. It's an old black and white film starring Brando, in his early hot years, before he let himself get fat and sloppy.

Inside the car I punch my father in the arm as hard as I can, but he doesn't flinch. I may as well be hitting a sand bag.

"Stop it, Dad."

My father chuckles and shakes his head, before returning to the program.

My mother looks at both of us.

"What'd I miss?"

"Nothing," I say. Part of me is embarrassed. The other part thinks it's about time she finds herself on the outside of an inside joke. Between my mother and sister, they have so many it almost seems like they have their own language.

My mother slows down in front of a larger white colonial home with black trim. Expansive green pastures flank the house and a For Sale sign is fixed in the grass out front.

"Look at this place, Paul," my mother says. She eases the window down and the scent of freshly cut alfalfa tumbles in.

Without thinking, I take a deep breath, then sneeze so hard it makes my father jump in his seat.

"She's allergic, June."

Compromising, my mother slides the window up midway.

For a while my parents see little else but that big white house. "They're asking a hundred and eighty-five," my mother informs him. "I heard the owners, a doctor and his wife, need to get out of Dodge quick. He botched a gastric bypass surgery and is about to lose his medical license. The poor woman didn't make it." My mother shakes her head in staged sympathy. Everything about this scene is an act, including how she just happened to choose this route from the airport. "I bet they'd take a hundred and a quarter."

The reality of hard numbers doesn't figure into my father's dream state. He focuses on the horse auction program again.

"We don't have that kind of liquid cash."

My mother pulls at the program like a not so playful game of tug of war. As with most head games, she wins.

"How do you plan on paying for whatever it is you've been salivating on in there?"

"The Tasakas trial." My father takes back the program. "I've got twenty or so to play with. That's all."

"So you did get the rapist off," my mother says. "I'm surprised you were able to slip out from beneath all that evidence." She's talking about Peter Tasakas, the single catch in his early thirties from our church who has single-handedly been caught with practically every female parishioner under the age of fifty, minus my mother. Even with his reputation or maybe because of it, the women rallied around Peter, and in order to help pay for his legal defense they threw a bake sale—baklava, powdery sugared Kourabiethes cookies, and olive bread. A woman in her forties, fresh from the homeland with a unibrow and a pair of man's hands, showed up at our door that night with an envelope stuffed with close to a grand in cash.

"Alleged rapist," my father corrects my mother. "Less than two hours the jury acquitted him. Why would a young, good-looking bachelor on the rise sexually assault a fat, ugly woman in his car in broad daylight? Everyone knows he could've done better. It only makes sense."

"That's why you're so good at what you do, honey." My mother leans across the console and for the first time in months, lightly touches her lips with his. "You know, a place like this might be a perfect investment for Beth Anne."

"Possibly."

My mother isn't giving up. She's been married long enough to a defense lawyer to know how to argue like one. "Please tell me," she says. "What might be the compensatory damages for a woman who's had her tubes tied without her consent?"

My father says nothing and I'm reminded of that night shortly after Nicholas came home when my mother broke out the F word, when I heard too much and couldn't get back to sleep.

Beth Anne is my father's wealthiest client, a woman who was supposedly driven crazy by her husband's verbal abuse. One night after a particularly high stakes yelling match over money, she took off in her car and was later found roadside in the Arizona desert having finally run out of gas. Her estranged husband claims he's never even raised his voice to her and she's simply gone off her meds. In the middle of an expensive divorce, she has been institutionalized again for what doctors have diagnosed as another nervous breakdown. Because she can no longer think straight my father signs all of her checks.

This big white house already haunts me. I fear my parents will want to buy this place. To my father, the house will be a refuge where he can get away temporarily from the stresses of his law practice. For my mother, it will be a refuge of her own, a permanent refuge away from him.

"I can't live out here in the sticks," I plead.

"Not everything is about you, Paula." My mother's small eyes shrink in the rearview mirror. Already this place has become too important to her. "Nothing has been decided yet. Your father and I are just *talking*."

* * *

The auction is held in a ritzy white barn at Lytle Creek Farms complete with canopies at either entrance, an open bar and crab cakes and fried shrimp for hors d'oeuvres. While my mother and sister search for seating in the stands, I head to the bar to see if I can score a glass of champagne. If I get caught I plan on explaining that I'm taking it outside to my father.

A super fan roars behind the bartender, whipping at his vest and parting his hair in strange places. He's busy mixing a drink for a woman who looks as if she's in her early forties. In equestrian chic, her silk dress runs wild, with horse heads all over it. She has on high heels, dry mud caked up half the spike. On her ring finger is a small fortune in diamonds shaped like a horseshoe.

For show I pour sparkling cider in a plastic cup, then fill another with champagne.

Racing down the middle of the barn aisle, an overweight woman in a dressy pant suit struggles to keep up with a spunky yearling. Her face is pumped up from the challenge as she halts on the heels of her boots, bends down, grabbing a fistful of dirt to sprinkle in front of the horse's eyes. Anything to get its ears to perk, but by the sound of the woman's huffing and puffing, instead of another handful of dirt she might next clutch her heart.

Perched in a box off to the side is the auctioneer, feverishly calling out numbers. "Five, five, give me five. I hear five." He sees something I don't and jabs his finger at a person in the stands. "No, six . . ." Before I can look who he pointed at, he's off again. He unleashes the same string of numbers so fast they echo into the next, adding up to pure confusion. I don't see how anybody is keeping up, or figuring out who bid what. A man in a button-down shirt and a greasy orange cap raises his paper wand with the number forty-five on it and nods.

The auctioneer strikes his program right at the mic for effect.

"Sold for sixty-five hundred!"

In the midst of all the clapping and hooting, I spot my mother and sister fitting tight in the first row. They're whispering about the next horse up for sale. Or rather, by the amused, almost dirty smiles on their faces, they're talking about its handler, a lanky man in his thirties with curly hair and enormous ears, a married man my sister will soon secretively lose her fear of men with. I don't imagine I'll be missed anytime soon.

On my way outside I toss the apple cider in the trash and sneak my father's car phone out of the mini-van. I don't want him catching me with it. The rates will be expensive from here to California.

There's no need to be concerned. He has my brother on his

shoulders, and his head is oddly tilted as he watches a horse, a two- or three- year-old stallion, throw out its front legs in a sweeping gait called the running walk.

"Now there's one high stepper," my father calls out.

The rider is Rhea's trainer, the Fly Bye owner's daughter. Her red curls are pulled back in a French braid, the kind of style my sister says only women who have none do with their long hair.

I dial Tomo's number and she actually picks up instead of her mother.

"Guess what I'm drinking." I take a fizzy sip and hold the stem, ladylike, between two fingers. "Champagne. They have an open bar and nobody's carding."

"Get enough buzz for the both of us."

Tomo doesn't sound impressed. Something's wrong and I sit on the rear bumper of a pick-up, ready to listen. What would be my good fortune she'd see as her bad luck if she and Jesse broke up. Because of him we hardly ever see each other.

"What's the matter?" I ask. My fingers are crossed in the hopes that Jesse is toast.

"I'm six weeks," she says.

For a moment I let it sink in, this news, even though I know perfectly well what she means. Why she's left out the word that must scare her the most, the word that when spoken will give life to what has been simply a measure of time. Over the line, her voice breaks.

Almost two thousand miles separate us, and I walk toward the other barn, the barn made out of cement blocks painted green with fake white shutters, where it'll be filled with show horses, but quiet. I'm hoping to hear her clearer, I'm hoping to get closer. The air inside is cool and smells like horses and strangely also like gasoline.

Down at the far end of the barn a groom is half-hidden in the shad-
ows, rubbing down a horse's front legs with a rag. What I smell isn't gas
but mustard oil used to burn through flesh so that the horse lifts higher,
its hooves practically on fire. The horse stomps, pawing from pain. The
torturous practice is illegal and cruel but no matter how many fines
and suspensions the federal government slaps these sadistic trainers with
when caught during inspection at horse shows, it nevertheless continues
to happen in the most exclusive barn aisles in the South. I can only hope
the groom with the rag will have to pee and forget to wash his hands first.

"Paula," Tomoko says. "You there?"

I turn back toward the way I came.

"Are you sure?" I ask lamely.

She doesn't answer, and I understand that she expects more from
me. She expects me to grow up.

"I need money," she finally says, "for my half."

"Should you tell your mom?"

"I don't need to."

It's true. The laws in California don't require parental consent.

Her family is Mormon, the practicing kind. They attend church
every Sunday. They do without coffee, alcohol, and even chocolate.
They do without other kinds of material things because there are so
many of them. They are the kind of family whose prayers must get an-
swered first or at least before the prayers of a family like mine that only
attends church for funerals, weddings, and the occasional bake sale for
a suspected rapist.

"My appointment is next Wednesday," Tomoko says.

"They make you wait a couple days in case you change your mind."

Feeling something isn't right, I stop, having stepped on something soft and fleshy with my flip-flop. Its rubbery tail is as thick as an extension cord. A decaying rodent the size of a small cat warrants a scream but I remember who I'm talking to and stifle it.

"All I have is forty-five," I blurt out, running from the dead rat. The champagne has left me lightheaded and heavy footed. Not to mention as I make it outside the wave of heat and moisture sucks the air right out of my lungs.

"I'll send it as soon as I can."

She sounds relieved though it probably has little to do with my few dollars. It's my emotional support she's after.

"Paula Girl," my father shouts. He's watched me this entire time, and if he's upset that I'm racking up the minutes on his car phone, he doesn't show it. Instead he extends his arm toward the young black stallion like a game show hostess showcasing a fully loaded Winnebago. "Meet the next World Grand Champion, Midnight's Secret Wish."

The redhead with the French braid is still on its back, only now she's holding my little brother up there, too, in a cowboy hat that's too big for his head and plastic six shooters at his side. A local reporter takes a picture with one of those clunky big bulb cameras for the *Shelbyville Gazette*. At two, this is Nicholas's first horseback ride, and I don't understand how my father could be so stupid. My mother is far smarter, and it's anyone's guess just how much it'll cost him when she comes across this picture, this memory, stolen from her by one of his female clients, in tomorrow's morning paper.

To make up for buying a forty-thousand-dollar two-year-old stallion yesterday at the auction, my father is about to place a bid for a one hundred and eighty-five thousand dollar home.

My father takes one last look at my mother.

"You sure about this, June?"

"Honey," she answers, sweetly, venomously. "It's perfect." She snakes her arms behind his neck and could just as easily turn on him if he goes against her. "Our own plantation. I've never been more sure of anything in my life."

"We're prepared to pay with cash," my father says to the realtor. "I'm assuming a cashier's check is okay?"

The realtor becomes flustered, excusing herself to place some calls.

My sister heads upstairs where there are two oversized rooms that expand across the entire length of the house.

"I call first dibs."

She beats me easily since I'm in charge of Nicholas and his toddler steps in Ninja Turtle tennis shoes are slowing me down. Once we reach the top, Nicholas pulls free so he can join in Rhea's excitement.

"This one's mine," my sister declares, choosing the room with the most amount of sunlight.

"That's not fair," I say. "You're just going to pull the drapes anyway and sleep."

Rhea seems pleased that I'm upset. "I'll be too busy to do much of that. I'll be running Dad's horse breeding business."

"He doesn't have one yet."

"That's why Mom and Dad are buying this place."

I shake my head.

"He's buying it so Mom won't be mad at him anymore," I say, anxious to point out I'm no longer out of the loop. "He's making up for having Dr. Simpkins perform that surgery so she can't have any more babies."

Rhea waves her hand at what has happened as if it has nothing to do with what's happening now. She's smug in how much she knows and I don't.

"That's just one of the reasons Mom wants to live out here."

My father was right on the drive to the hospital in Long Beach about the horses serving as a distraction for Rhea. They've given her confidence, almost to the point of arrogance. They've also brought the two of them closer, this dream they share of being major players in the Walking Horse industry. And I'm jealous. I'm jealous I've lost my summers with my father at Anaheim Stadium. It's the only place he and I actually enjoyed going together and looked forward to and now it was slipping away like so many other things between us. Without a second thought he gave up our season seats so he could afford to buy an entire box for the family at the ten-day Walking Horse National Celebration.

"Dad's moving the horses out here to Fletcher Wilson's barn," Rhea explains.

"The dude who looks like Dumbo?"

My sister licks her lips, and I'm curious how many guys she's French kissed or if, like Tomo, she's done far more with her mouth.

"You know what they say about men with big ears."

Before landing my punch line, I inch toward the stairs.

"They're a convenient place for a slut like you to rest her feet?"

Because of past arguments, my reflexes are sharp. I know to duck as she pulls off her riding boot and pitches it straight for me. The heel part leaves a lasting impression in the wall, cracking the plaster. I escape down the stairs so I won't be blamed, ditching Nicholas up there with her.

My father pokes his head into the foyer.

"What the hell's going on?"

I shrug.

"Rhea's letting Nick run wild." I lie in the hopes my sister will think twice about telling him the truth. If he finds out about her crush, he would likely abort all plans of letting Dumbo be her new trainer. "Let me go home with you next week," I say. "If I stay here I'm just going to get in the way. You know I will." Still there are more reasons and I throw everything at him except the kitchen sink and the riding boot Rhea just threw at me. "Besides, you'll get lonely."

Maybe it's something in my voice my father finally hears. He knows me best and can sense when things aren't right. It's not just about Tomo. My bad attitude about this house goes against how good the rest of the family feels about it. None of them could be any happier.

Both of my parents come from a place where I haven't, a place where they've gone without. As a girl my mother couldn't afford new shoes and slipped in strips of cardboard for soles. My father brought home the damaged fruit from his job delivering produce like his late father had so the family would have something other to eat at breakfast than oatmeal. More than just a second home, this colonial estate in Tennessee is a measure of how far they've come. It is their common need to separate themselves from their ghetto roots in L.A. that threatens to separate them from each other.

"What's wrong, Paula Girl?"

"Nothing, I just want to go back home with you when you leave."

"That's it?"

The question runs a lot deeper than he could possibly figure out. The horses, the house, all of it's coming too quickly. My father taught me that everything has its price and, in retrospect, I don't know why he couldn't see that there was something his cashier's check hadn't covered. Or maybe he mistakenly thought that in his wife's eyes, by buying her this beautiful house, he was somehow raising his own worth.

WHAT THEY TOLD ME AFTER HE DIED

If we're talking about the same sweet Sugar, she dances to old Prince songs. "Get Off" and "Cream" are her favorites. I mean *used to be*. She doesn't work here anymore. Up and quit a couple nights ago. Right before she was supposed to go on. Stiffed the stiffs, if you know what I mean.

—Erica, dancer at the Kat Nip

There is no police report on file. Sounds like there's something more you're leaving out, Miss. Men like the one you're describing don't show up on these streets at that time of night unless they're looking to score.

—Officer Peterson, Compton Police

Your dad loved you more than anything, Paula. You know that. The rest, you're best off not knowing.

—Lucia, my best friend

You two were like a little team.

—Lola, Uncle Dimitri's girlfriend

He called and told me he knew that stripper chick was behind it. He actually referred to her as his girlfriend. Apparently, he wasn't thinking too clearly. She had another boyfriend, a real one. The whole thing was a set-up. Dad said she watched it all go down from inside the house. He said he saw her close the front door. I don't know why he wouldn't tell you. Maybe he was afraid you'd hunt her down or something.

—Rhea Priamos

I told you, she doesn't work here anymore.

—Erica

Please, Paula. Baby, have another Valium, for me.

—Jim Brown, my fiancé

RED EYE

The plane ride home is night-and-day different from our trip to Tennessee, seeing the pre-dawn detour we take to the Hawaiian island of Oahu. My father has some papers that need signing, more property he's purchasing, as if the colonial estate and the two year old stallion he's just bought aren't enough. His spending spree has been non-stop from the first class flight to Nashville, and now as we hover thirty thousand feet above the Pacific, he tells me what he'll be snapping up next.

"Soon I'm going to build a hotel, Paula Girl," he rushes on, his arms waving at all his big plans that are right outside that tiny window. The sky is silvery dark and limitless, lightening with the prospect of the day ahead. "Everybody buys property on the coast, but really, what's the point? Why not build a great big one inland? These islands are so small. If you build high enough, every room will have a goddamn view."

It won't be until I'm well into my twenties and well into an affair with a man who tries and drowns out this same kind of erratic energy with alcohol that I'll understand my father was probably bipolar. Too stubborn to ever seek treatment, he believed only women and men who were nothing but weak-kneed *kariolis* relied on therapy and pills for something a real man could work clean out in his own head. Never will he recognize the high he's experiencing now buying unaffordable things nor the low he'll suffer later once he's caught and forced to relinquish them all. Denial runs in the family. He'll pathologically deny he's done anything wrong in the same vein that his own blood refuses to acknowledge one of their members is a well armed, full blown pedophile.

In my father's frenzied state it's hard not to get caught up along with him—the possibility that we may actually one day move to the Paradise State. If I'm not as curious as I should be why I'm told not to mention the property to my mother, I at least ask.

"She's too focused on the farm," my father says, brushing it off. "I'll tell her soon enough. This trip is last minute. But I thought, what the hell. We're already in the air anyway, right Paula Girl?"

On the descent the expanse of blue waters is so clear I can see the tangles of coral beneath.

For a last minute trip, he planned in a jam fairly well, considering a rental car is waiting for us when we hit the terminal. Pierre is flown ahead to Ontario, where he apparently won't have to wait for very long. We're only staying the day on the island, catching a late night flight.

My father drops me off at the Sheraton on the beach of Waikiki, where I'm to pretend I'm a guest. He's taking a chopper to an even more lush and rural island called Molokai. Before he goes, he buys me a bamboo mat, an old lady one piece swimsuit, a ticket to the all-you-can-eat breakfast buffet, and hands me a fifty.

"Don't leave the beach. Don't call your mother, and don't forget to tip big. We don't want the locals thinking we're cheap tourists."

To make him happy, I recite his art of tipping rules. "Always match the amount of the check."

When he returns a few hours later he takes us to an early dinner at a high end restaurant by the water called Don Domenic's, known for its exotic salt water pond sprinkled with plumeria petals, where every meal is a fresh catch of the day. It is from this pond we choose our dinner. My father decides on a scuttling lobster and I select calamari because squid is not only ugly sounding but with no fins or claws it's the least realistic form of sea life I can find. After our meal he pays with cash, leaving behind an outrageous gratuity, a C-note, which inspires our waiter to escort us, with many thanks, all the way out of the restaurant.

On the flight back to Ontario, my father can't stop talking about the young horse he bought at the auction. It's as if our side trip to Hawaii hasn't happened, and if I hadn't packed away the proof, the ceramic Buddha from my Virgin Strawberry Daiquiri I'd drank while tanning on the beach, I'd suspect it hadn't either.

"You know why he's going to be a champion?"

Patiently, I take off my headphones. The least I can do is listen since he persuaded my mother to let me go home with him. It didn't take much, just a promise I'd be back before late August when the Celebration begins and my seat in the Priamos box needs to be filled.

"Why?"

"Because he jumped out of the trailer. *Jumped*." My father slides his hands together, then apart in a liftoff motion. "Only a horse with heart does that."

Or one that's frightened and wants out, I want to say but don't.

"How'd you get the money for the rest?" I ask. "You told Mom you only had twenty thousand from the Tasakas trial."

My father looks startled like he did when I told him I thought Bared wasn't crazy.

"My checkbook is my business, not yours."

To lighten up the dark mood I put him in, I lean forward in my seat and bend my arms as if I'm about to squawk like a chicken.

"I could get used to flying with so much elbow room."

My father smiles, finishing off his Jack Daniels on the rocks. Unfortunately ouzo, his favorite hard liquor, has yet to make the cocktail menu on American Airlines flights. Showing affection never comes easily. His pats on my back are more like thuds, and when he does it now I accidentally swallow the Life Saver I'd been sucking on.

"First class from now on, Paula Girl," he says. "You may want to get some sleep so you'll look your best for *Viva Zapata*."

Faking annoyance, I roll my eyes, then replace my headphones.

"Enough with the bad Spanish, Dad."

Suddenly, he appears serious. Now that we're circling back to Ontario, flying over the dry desert of the Mojave, over more familiar ground, we're too close to home for things to be funny anymore. The joke is over.

"It's okay if that boy comes around again," my father says, pointing. "But the porch light stays on."

I pop out my cassette tape, switching sides.

"It's not like Cheech would ever hurt me. He isn't exactly a rapist."

"And how would you know what he's capable of?" My father's face hardens in reaction to the shot bottle of liquor he's drank, in reaction to what I've just said. "It doesn't matter who he is or how old. If he has good grades or bad ones. If he's got money or is dead ass broke but with a heart of gold. A guy will always want more than you're willing to give."

I think of Tomoko and almost tell him of the fix she's in. Then I think twice.

"You mean like what happened to that poor woman who got into Peter Tasakas's car?"

"It was his word against hers, and he's been acquitted."

"Still, he could be a rapist."

"Maybe," my father says this like he may believe it too. "But don't twist shit around, Paula Girl. I defend the accused. Sometimes I defend lowlife. It's not my place to judge."

"Right," I say. "It's just your job to get them off."

"No piece of shit *nothos* like Peter Tasakas, much less that little shit next door, will ever put his hands all over one of my daughters. You hear me?"

There is no point in trying to talk to my father once he starts in with the hypothetical threats, the Greek curse words, the Lynwood ghetto in him that no amount of money or degrees or colonial estates on thirty acres of countryside will ever separate him from.

In another row, a woman wearing a muu muu and a wilting lei around her neck is appalled at my father's foul language. Her pupils are like bullseyes, the whites overly pronounced.

I bug mine out too until she quits staring.

"Jesus, Dad," I whisper, humiliated as much at my own bad behavior as his. "Everybody in first class heard you."

Virginity is saved like a souvenir in my family. It's a Greek tradition on the young couple's wedding night for the husband to use a white handkerchief and stain it with the bride's blood after lovemaking. In his sock drawer, in embroidered lace sewn by my yia yia, my father still keeps the symbol of my mother's purity.

*　*　*

The abortion clinic is in Montclair, a block away from the hospital where my mother delivered Nicholas. I ride in the backseat of Jesse's immaculate BMW. Hanging from the rearview mirror is a scented air freshener in the shape of a banana that smells like laundry detergent. I remember something my father says to warn me off dating. "Never trust a guy whose car is too clean. A sure sign he wants to keep you in it too long." Cheech's car reeks of French fries. Fast food wrappers and his baseball cleats have to be shoved off the passenger seat just so I can sit down.

I've only been home for less than a day, and Cheech has no idea I'm back. For now, I want to keep it that way.

It's hard not to imagine how many times Jesse parked this old car somewhere dark and remote. How many times he must've reclined the passenger's seat and lay so much weight on Tomo, pressuring her to just let him in, to just let him love her. How many times she must've resisted before finally giving in.

Tomo is quick getting out of the car. Jesse isn't. On the outside, he's as pristine as this glorified junker he likes to call a classic. His black hair is purposely messy and his t-shirt is bright white like it's been ripped straight out of the package. Underneath is where he's missing all the right parts.

He pulls out a pack of Marlboros and punches in his cigarette lighter.

I'd like to punch his face. Intentionally, I throw his seat forward, pushing my way out of the car from his side.

"Hey," he says, his body squeezed at the wheel. "A head's up might be nice."

I lean near him.

"Tomo could've used one of those when she first met you."

I'm her best friend and Jesse must know better than to say anything back. Maybe he simply doesn't care.

"I'll wait out here for you, babe," he says to Tomo while lighting up. "The smell of hospitals makes me sick."

Tomo is inside for over an hour before I pull out a book. Instead of a Jackie Collins novel, the kind I usually read, filled with too much sex and money, I have with me Hemingway's *Old Man and the Sea*, a story about a man catching a fish.

I'm finished with the short novel by the time Tomo reappears from behind the waiting room door. Mascara and eye shadow smear dark at the corners of her eyes as if she's tried to cover up a good cry. Her hair is ironed straight and slick when it looks better fluffy and coarse to the touch. Another one of Jesse's suggestions.

Her hand rests small on the flat of her stomach. She smiles weakly, and I see how badly she could use her mother's strength. All those years I spent disliking the woman for not liking me because I'm white seem pointless. She was only trying to protect her little girl, and, as it turns out, both of our defenses were aimed at the wrong person.

"They don't tell you how much it hurts afterward," Tomo says. "They leave that part out."

Prematurely I get the door, waiting there, unsure if I should put my arm around her or just stay close. In the heat outside I realize it doesn't matter. The distance is already there between us. Bound by this secret she will keep from her family, I'll only serve as a reminder of what she's done.

While I don't know it then, in less than two weeks she will break off the relationship with Jesse, though what is left behind is much harder to end. Far into adulthood, well after she is married and bears two healthy sons, Tomo will continue to mark her abortion as a morbid kind of birthday, speculating how old the child would've been had she let it live.

* * *

Cheech is working beneath the black hood of his car when Tomo and Jesse drop me off. His St. Christopher's baseball cap is on backward. Shocked to see me, he lets the hood slam down.

I wave, but he doesn't wave back. His eyes are only on Jesse.

"You want to stay the night?" I ask Tomo. This time I get out on her side, lightly brushing her shoulder. "My dad's meeting with a client at the L.A. prison. He won't be home for hours. You can have Rhea's room."

At first it looks as if Tomo is tempted, but Jesse has too much control down to her most vital parts.

Between the heavy make-up and the way she's staring straight ahead, I'm unable to read her.

Jesse leans over.

"She's hanging with me tonight. We're kicking it at my buddy's house. You know, play some pool."

He gestures with his chin toward the Murillo house.

"Who's the wetback?"

"Go to hell, Jesse," I say, swinging shut the passenger door so hard he winces. "He's lighter than you."

As Jesse backs out of the drive, Cheech meets me halfway between our two homes on the bridle path. He wipes his hands on a dirty rag and tucks it in his back pocket.

"How come you didn't tell me you were back?"

"I didn't have time," I say. It's a lame excuse given he's just caught me driving up with my friend.

He nods toward my house and smiles.

"The Godfather home?"

I laugh a little.

"Not yet. He's at the prison talking to a murderer or something." I notice I don't tell him the prison in L.A. He probably assumes Chino, which is just as well. I don't want to invite him in. I don't want to be alone with him for that long.

"Where's yours?"

"My mom and dad are at Rigo's game."

The sun is almost gone, and the street lights are flickering. I tell myself not to worry. My father couldn't be home for hours, not even if he left the prison right now, speeding down the emergency lane with his lights flashing. Pierre cries for me by the side gate leading to the pool.

Gently Cheech pulls me into his arms, and I smell the sweat and the grease, the hours he's spent working on his car. I wonder if he loves it the same way Jesse does his.

"I'm glad you're back."

He touches the side of my face and I lean in because I've been waiting long before that night on the porch.

We kiss, soft and slow. I feel his kiss everywhere, down in my chest, then between my legs. Soon his mouth moves more urgently on mine. His tongue pushes hot and wet at my lips, wanting in. I try and pull back. He won't let me. His hands hold me in place, and I feel it there against my leg, just how hard the other part of him wants to get inside me too.

"Stop." My voice sounds too loud like he's hurting me.

Cheech doesn't listen. He nuzzles my neck and starts backing me up toward my driveway, toward my sister's 280 Z, and I know what he's bracing me for.

My father had been worried on the plane ride home of this situation, when I find myself alone with a guy who wants too much.

This time I make myself heard. I push Cheech back hard, forcing enough space so that he might not ever try it again.

FAMISHED FRAT BOYS

My mother gives it to me straight over a pastrami on rye that she's leaving my father for good. This is at the drive-thru at a sub shop called The Old Hat. I'm sixteen and it's the fall of my junior year. She has picked the most opportune time to make her big move. The horse show season is over and Tennessee is most welcoming this time of year. Unlike California there are four seasons, not just two. There are green leaves, golden leaves, orange leaves, trees that have shed them all, icy streets, and tornado watches. Even the weather is more eventful.

"I wanted to tell you in case you decide to come with us." Us. That word automatically excludes me and it's never included my father.

"Where's Dad?"

"At work." My mother sighs as if my asking about him is expected, predictable like The Old Hat neon sign that spins high above. We're in the parking lot. Apparently she was worried I'd make the same scene inside the fast food joint that I'm making outside in her car. "It would be too hard for him to see the movers."

"Movers?"

"Honey." My mother reaches out for me but I'm too quick and I open the door and lean out. I drop the sandwich, soggy with mayonnaise, with mustard. She can't even remember that I eat mine dry. "I meant what I said," she continues. "I'm leaving your father. We haven't been happy for some time. You should come with me. Your father," she says. "He isn't stable. He's done some bad things. He's spent money that isn't his."

I don't want to eat, but I do cry. "Only because you stopped loving him," I say, talking back in a way I never have to her before. "He bought you that stupid house so you wouldn't go." Sobs rack my chest, and I heave and hiccup, and right then it makes perfect sense that if she can stop loving him, I can just as easily stop loving her.

My mother knows not to touch me. If she does I might strike out at her, I might slap and scratch that smooth porcelain doll skin she inherited from the Irish side in her mother. She starts the car and drives out of the lot. Her expression is stoic, but behind it is the possibility of a new life nearly two thousand miles away from the one we've built here.

"Your secret trip to Hawaii that the two of you think I don't know about? Who do you think paid for that?" My mother shakes her head. She still has time. We're at a stoplight. "His clients will catch on. It's only a matter of when."

* * *

The moving van is parked out front of the house, the back of it wide open, the ramp slanted in place. Strapped against one side is the dining room hutch, with no pink floral plates stacked inside, no wedding silver, partially covered with a quilted blanket to protect it for the two day trip ahead. Two college aged guys with bloated beer bellies appear, each carrying an end of my old mattress, the one my mother slept on while Nick was a baby, the same one at four years old he's now grown into. The chubby movers wear dusty black t-shirts that read *Famished Frat Boys* in hazard orange.

As I watch them lift and slide the mattress in the back, leaning it against the hutch, I know I'll remember their t-shirts, how unfunny they are. How stupid the two of them are for wearing them. How they stink. I'll remember how startled they appear at my face that is temporarily disfigured, that's raw and swollen from the verbal blows my mother blindsided me with in the car.

She has given me less than forty-five minutes to make my decision. To point these same movers toward my bedroom. But I don't. I can't. I can only think of my father, what he might do if all he has to come home to is the bottle of ouzo he keeps on top of the freezer. I'm afraid that the loaded Savage he keeps upright in his walk-in closet will be all the more visible now that the closet is half-empty. I'm afraid my leaving will give him ammo.

Dropping to my knees out on the front lawn under the cooling sun, there aren't words painful enough to hurt her with. But I do find one she won't soon forget.

"Fuck you, Mom," I say to her, my scream so internal and instinctual, like a wounded animal, that one of the movers lets go of something fragile. "Fuck you," I say again, "and fuck our family."

*   *   *

My father's office is less than a mile away in a one story duplex that looks more like low income housing. The inside is even worse, with burnt shag carpet and seventies style wood paneling. I drive the Z, Rhea's old car that has now been handed down to me. The muffler kicks out a couple puffs of smoke at stoplights whenever I hit the gas. Once the new meds leveled Rhea's moods my parents found it safe to give her a brand new customized gold 325 I BMW with a sun roof and tan leather seats.

The diesel Mercedes is the only car still in the lot. His secretary has gone home for the day. It's getting late, dinner time. I call out for him but he doesn't answer. The door to his office is closed, and when I enter, the room is dark. He is not seated at his desk, cluttered with the manila folders stuffed with legal documentation of other peoples' problems. I find him lying face down on the floor as if reenacting the death pose of a victim from a crime scene photo. I have never seen him so hurt, so beaten down.

I flip on the light.

"What are you doing?"

"Nothing," he says. He rubs at his face roughly with his hands. "I was just resting."

"Then get up." My voice is stern, a teenage daughter scolding her grown father. I know no other way. "They're gone," I say, "and I'm hungry. I haven't eaten since lunch."

Most of these things are lies but he believes me, maybe because I'm all he has left, and I shut the door when I hear him getting up so he can collect himself.

* * *

For some reason my father wants to drive the Z, and on the way to Yanni's for dinner in Claremont, we say very little. The shock of it all is too enormous, too much like death. Right before we turn onto Indian Hill Boulevard, my father veers instead toward the auto center. Ford. Toyota. Chrysler. Shiny SUV's, single cab trucks, and sports cars angle out in every direction.

"Dad," I say. "What are we doing here?"

My father points to the cluster of men standing under a tent at the Nissan dealership, wearing business shirts and ties, no jackets.

"Tell me, Paula Girl. Which one of those *poutsakis* do you think will come over here first?"

My stomach is jittery from all that I've lost today, the one huge thing I might drive off with this evening.

"You're serious?" I ask. "You're actually going to buy me a car?"

I'd reach over and hug him but I'm afraid touching him might break the spell. As it is, his smile doesn't look right. None of this does, yet I'm not about to turn down a brand new car. When it comes to hard cash my father either has too much of it or he's flat broke.

A gray-haired guy heads right for us, rolling down his sleeves and buttoning the cuffs. He sees me in the car, the defeated look on my father's face, the near giddy look on mine, my eyes puffy from crying. He smells our spilled blood.

"Deal is," my father says as we get out. "You buy something on the showroom floor, tonight. No questions. No special orders. Now. You understand?"

I nod, and before he changes his mind, I sail right past the salesman and through the automatic doors to the showroom floor. And there it is—an off white sports car, a coupe, two door, with a tail fin in the back and a spoiler in the front. I've seen the commercials for it on TV. An unidentified man is driving. Riding shotgun is a Cover Girl supermodel.

"An affordable sports car that's so sleek even she will ride in it." Through a side window I peer in. The interior is fabric, charcoal gray. I picture my friend Lucia in the passenger seat, the two of us flying into the student parking lot. All heads will turn, even Big Bird's, the female narc.

"That's a new model, the 240 SX," the dealer explains. "We're not getting our first shipment for another couple months. This one isn't for sale."

I open the driver's side and slide in.

"It's even an automatic, Dad." I don't drive stick, never learned. My father says there's no point in coordinating all that hand and foot work at every stop and start in Southern California gridlock.

From the side mirror, I see my father's dark eyes come back to life because of me, my excitement. He's pulling out his checkbook and it now makes sense why he brought me here. With my mother on her way to Tennessee, he's clearing out their joint bank account before she does it for him. I'm flattered he'd rather spend the money on me than stuff it in his mattress or blow it on another horse.

"How much?" he presses the dealer. "My daughter wants this one, not next month, but now, tonight."

The salesman looks around like he needs help, like my father might be a real nut job, his best customer yet.

"I'll have to discuss it with my manager."

My father rips out a blank check.

"Call my bank."

He is in no mood to make deals, not while his wife is behind the wheel of a moving van, taking one of his children, another following closely behind in her own car, more than halfway across the country. They're probably already past California state lines, well into the scrub brush and fragrant Saguaro cactus in the Arizona desert.

"I find it hard to believe there's any car in this lot that's not for sale, including the one you drove here to work."

And my father's right. There isn't. Less than a half hour it seems my father has traded in the Z and we're pulling out onto the street in my brand new ivory 240 SX, the sticker price and car's special features still taped to the rear side window.

"Give it some gas, Paula Girl," he encourages me as we speed past the Nissan dealership, the stunned salesman we dealt with still standing out front. "Say aloha to the *poutsaki* who nearly blew his commission by following the rules."

This is my father's way of letting me in on where he has found the money for my car by selling the Molokai property, by selling it right out from under my mother. As a defense lawyer he presumes nobody is ever telling him everything, which is why no matter how much it hurt, he must've suspected for a while now that his wife was leaving. The car moves fast like the Z and I take the first corner sharp, blowing through a yellow light. My father puts down his window yet I leave mine up. The reward for staying with him is bittersweet, a hundred and forty horse power strong. On this night it is understood between my father and me that this may only be a test drive and I will get this exact same car, if not right then, than soon enough when his check eventually clears. How I wanted to breathe in, for just a little while longer, the new car smell.

WHAT THEY TOLD ME AFTER HE DIED

Beth Anne's husband had it out for your father like nobody's business. He'd call the office, drop by, sometimes even warn clients before they walked in. Harassment is what it was. The s.o.b. did everything but hand your father a bottle of pills and a glass of water.

—Nora, legal assistant

He always told me he loved me. Right before we'd hang up, he always said it.

—Rhea Priamos

Your father's life was destroyed years ago the day he got together with that half-breed. It just sickens me. All my sons chose to marry the wrong women.

—Yia Yia

He didn't think I was really leaving. That day when the movers showed up, he went to the office like it was any other day. He thought I was bluffing. Too many years spent ignoring the evidence.

—June Priamos

A woman is supposed to outlive her husband, not her child. What am I supposed to do?

—Yia Yia

Your yia yia sews voodoo dolls out of tube socks and uses thumb tacks for the eyes. I came across them once in her dresser. I was looking for a sweater because I was cold. Being raised by a mother who holds onto so much hate, it's no wonder your father never knew how to love me.

—June Priamos

I just keep thinkin' back to why Uncle Gil was in Dad's room in the first place. Hell, at that hour, I mean it was earlier than the chickens even think to roost.

—Nick Priamos

Gil suffers from an Oedipus complex, among others. He's Greek, isn't he? How else would you describe a man who'd rather live with his mother than his own wife. Who knows what really goes on in that family. Maybe your yia yia is to blame.

—June Priamos

Suicide? *I didn't say that.*

—Nora

You think I'm hiding something? Go ahead, Paula. Why don't you write about it.

—Psycho Gil

BIG BIRD AND OTHER FOUL TYPES

Someone is breaking into our house. The sound of shattered glass wakes me. Groggily, I sit up in bed. I listen. All balled up at the foot of my bed, Pierre snoozes on. He's getting too long in the tooth and deaf in the ears to be much of a watch dog anymore. But I know what I heard. It came from my bedroom window, only I'm two doors away, in my sister's old room. I've taken hers over since last year when they left.

Heavy footsteps pound down the hall.

"Paula Girl," my father yells. "You all right?"

I climb out of bed and meet him at the door. At his side is his trusty Savage. It doesn't seem he's figured out there is no bullet in the chamber. Right after my mother left I hid all the ammo to his hunting rifles between my mattress and bed spring.

"What happened?" I ask.

My father acts like he doesn't hear me, and switches on the light in my old room, walking in barefoot. Between the shards of glass lay what was tossed through the window—a metal horseshoe.

From the doorway, I stand shivering, my arms folded at my chest.

Whoever did this could be right outside.

"Dad," I say. "We'd better call the cops."

Boldly, my father yanks up the blinds, but there is nothing to confront except his own reflection, fractured in the glass. He turns.

"Cops only show up to stand around the dead bodies. No sense in getting them out here over a fucked up prank. Besides, it could've been anybody."

"Right," I say, "anybody with access to horseshoes."

I think of the defendants whose cases my father failed to win, the prosecutors who've lost their cases to him, the victims who never saw any justice. Psycho Gil. There are too many suspects to count. Just last week we developed a stalker, the disgruntled ex-husband of one of my father's clients whom I caught cruising by our home. My father says it's nothing—the man simply got the addresses of the house and office mixed up, but now I'm not so sure.

"You know how easy it would be for somebody to hop our fence and find one in the dirt?" my father points out. "I haven't seen *Viva Zapata* around lately."

His lawyer tactics anger me, the way he flips things around like this is somehow my fault.

"Cheech didn't do it."

Although he may still live next door, he's long since moved on from me. I've seen his new girlfriend—a striking Latina with long dark hair and penciled in brows. She attends an all-girls school. They're a match made in Catholic heaven.

My throat hurts, like I can't swallow, I can't speak, and I put a hand to my neck.

"I feel like I'm getting sick."

"Stay in the hallway," my father orders. "I don't want you back in your bedroom yet."

No matter how hard he tries to hide it, hurling a horseshoe through my window has him thrown. Before sending me back to bed, he breaks down a couple of cardboard boxes from the garage, taping one across the broken window. For safe measure he secures the other against my sister's. Then he makes a quick trip to the kitchen for an aspirin and a glass filled with orange juice on ice.

"Drink this," he says. "It's a Greek remedy for colds."

He's gone before I take the first sip, before I feel the burn, the hot taste of licorice, and I cough. To shut me up, my father has spiked my juice with ouzo.

* * *

The next morning when I leave for school, I find the ex-husband in the Cadillac parked across the street. He's baiting my father. He wants my father to know it was him. The horseshoe through the window must've been a message only the two of them would understand.

The windows are darkened and I watch as the driver's side rolls up. He does it to keep me from getting a good look or more likely to avoid the dairy smell. It makes me smile a little, the thought that the reek of agriculture, of cows and muck is getting to him. This is Chino in the late eighties and it won't take long for developers from Los Angeles to buy up and build over most of the fertile soil. Strip malls and new tract homes have pushed back the dairies, the strawberry fields, and horse farms to the outskirts toward rural Corona, though all it takes is a damp morning like this to serve as a reminder that farmland is just a few miles down the way.

Although I've never seen this man's face, I know who he is. He's the reason for a lot of things that have gone wrong around here. He's the reason why my father now buys bottles of ouzo in bulk from the island of Lesvos and keeps them on top of the freezer. He's the reason why my dad gets drunk, then stays up late, calculating columns and columns of numbers on a legal pad, figuring that if he keeps at it long enough the numbers will somehow add up right. He is what finally drove my mother to pack up my little brother and Rhea and caravan nearly two thousand miles away to move into our second home in Tennessee for good. She needed to protect what was rightfully hers.

Ignoring a Cadillac that's the size of a pontoon boat takes some doing as I get into the front seat and warm up my own car. The newness of my car, of our lives without the rest of the family, has worn off and my father thinks it's necessary that I see my sister's former shrink. I have an appointment next Friday. This will make my third visit and hopefully my last. I plan on making it memorable. My father says I need someone to talk to about losing my family since he knows he can't bear to hear it himself.

As I pull out of the driveway, the Cadillac creeps closer. He has plans to take my spot, and as I straighten the wheel, I see him clearly, head on, through the windshield. His gold-rimmed glasses. His mustache twisted up like an old-fashioned barber's at the ends.

He's eating a glazed donut. He has all day to wait because he's short of some things far more valuable than time. He's short on cash, on assets, on patience. My father represented Beth Anne, this man's wife, and now, right after their divorce was final, she drives around in a customized Jaguar, its seats covered with a special resilient leather so that her three Himalayan cats can travel with her. With some ingenious digging, my father unearthed several million dollars' worth of land and a condominium complex the wife never knew existed. After finding out my father has power of attorney over her fortune, the ex-husband has something to prove, to prove my father is no better at keeping his hands off her funds. I remember the cashier's check for the country estate I've coined the *Hee Haw* house, paid in full. It occurs to me that if I swerve right, I could watch him choke on that last bit. Hitting the man will just cause more problems for my father, problems he doesn't need, so instead of pressing down on the gas, I hold my hand up to the side window, flipping him off as I pass.

Something flashes inside his car. The freak has just taken my picture.

* * *

On my way to school I pick up my friend Lucia who lives around the corner. I honk and she comes out wearing her hair pulled back in a strange netting with a bow on top. She looks like a dressed up cafeteria lady. She wants to be an actress but being a pale Portuguese makes her a tough sell. Because she isn't attractive in the Malibu blond sense, an exotic Hawaiian suntan queen, or the cute girl next door sort of way, she invents a new image to give an edge to her looks. She has a black and white head shot and has gone on auditions. A couple years before she had one call back. It was for a movie about girl scouts, though she wound up not getting the part because at fourteen they said she looked too old.

I point to her head.

"I like it," I say. "What is it?"

Lucia touches the hair netting. Her dishwater curls bunch up like caught fish.

"A snood," she says, getting in. "They wore them in the forties or fifties."

Because her hair is so thin, so fine, the barrette part is already sliding.

"It's glamorous," I lie.

* * *

The student parking lot expands between the music building and the gym. Big Bird, the security guard, stands watch at the only way in to campus. She earned the nickname well before I ever attended this high school because her face is birdlike, too small for the rest of her body, and her belly barrels out just like the yellow feathered character from Sesame Street. She wears a policeman's mirrored shades and drab brown pants.

She's a narc, plain and simple. Everyone is supposed to make fun of her. No one even knows her real name.

"Paula!"

I turn.

It's Trevor.

He's captain of the varsity baseball team. A player way out of my league. I like the way he shouts my name with enthusiasm. He must be used to people saying his name that way from high up in the stands.

"So this is your 'mobile."

I nod.

Recently on a bet with his dad, he shaved the number sixteen, his team number, in the back of his head.

Sometimes before I go to bed I lay there, imagining what it would be like to curl up into him, to make out with him for so long—just make out, no rounding second plate, no sliding into home—that my neck stiffens like whiplash.

His eyes are green, his hair a dark blond.

Lucia gets out and leaves without saying goodbye. His popularity scares off most everybody, except those in his circle.

While I'm not in his circle, I'm definitely on his radar. Nearly a month before I ran into him in the quad during history class. I dropped my hall pass, the most unsanitary restroom pass in the entire school, a giant plastic toilet seat. It split right in two from the hinge part where it connects to the lid.

Trevor laughed, and it was the way he laughed that made me realize almost four years at the same school didn't matter. Finally and by accident, he was seeing me for the first time.

"Good job. Now where's Mr. Billings going to sit his ass down during lunch?"

As a side benefit of being the star of the baseball team, Trevor was acting T.A. to a non-existent woodshop class, which was supposed to give him time to do his homework. Instead he trolled the halls. Trevor took the toilet seat back to the room, and using vise grips, he superglued the split to a mere hairline fracture. What happened stayed a secret, a stupid one, though it was something that kept the two of us smiling at each other in passing for weeks to come.

Through the gates, as we pass Big Bird, Trevor tips the bill of his baseball cap. If anyone else tried this it would look like a pointed insult, but when Trevor does it, he actually gets a nod of acknowledgment from her.

Big Bird glances from him to me. Through those reflector shades it's annoying not to know how much of us she must see.

"Better get to class, Short Stop."

Maybe she says this in reference to his position out on the field or she could mean my temporary position in Trevor's life. I imagine she's seen him with tons of girls, including Becky Barton, the energetic and easy junior cheerleader. She's done everything to get his attention, even spraying his team number on the rear window of her car with that flocking spray used during Christmas.

Being "easy" sexually is apparently nothing to be ashamed of in our high school. Becky even advertises it on her license plate frame: Blondes tease. Redheads please.

Behind us, I hear Big Bird padlocking the gate, locking us in. The quad is emptying out, students scattering in all directions for their classes.

Unfortunately everybody is settling in their seats and nobody spots me being walked to class by Trevor except for Mr. Duvane, who is at the door. Holding it open for me isn't a chivalrous act. More like a sign I'm a couple seconds late.

He's only in his early forties and dresses like a senior citizen—pleated polyester pants, rubber soled lace-ups. The one feature that stands out the most on Mr. Duvane is his white man's 'fro. This, paired with his grandpa wear and thermos he keeps on his desk that's rumored to reek of vodka, prevents most students from asking for help after school.

His face is serious as his 'fro dips in the direction where Trevor took off.

"It's a good thing you look the way you do, Paula. With your bad grades, you'll need to marry someone like him." He touches my arm as he closes the door, and I turn because I don't want to smell what I suspect is on his breath. I don't want to know the reason he feels so at ease talking to me this way.

What Mr. Duvane says hits me hard, though I refuse to let him see how much. He has no clue why I've been distracted, why when I've studied, I can't remember a thing.

"I take it I didn't pass the test."

"You received sixty-seven percent."

My seat is in the back of the room, the cheap seats, Lucia and I call them. When I sit down, she pokes me with her pen. I know what she wants. She wants to hear the details about my walk with Trevor. In light of my D on the last test, I ignore her. I'm in enough trouble without getting caught talking.

Mr. Duvane begins going over what will be on the final. The only rows that seem to get his full attention are the first two, the university bound students. Harvard. Stanford. UCLA. Many of them have already been accepted to the school of their choice. Kimberly Foley, the rumored valedictorian, wears her maroon and yellow USC sweatshirt to class, refusing to take it off even when the room is uncomfortably hot.

In all fairness, where I fall behind in his class is more my fault than his. At the beginning of the semester I could've insisted on sitting closer. I could've shown up after school and asked for help. Even if he was trashed, at least he'd know I came to him. It's too late now. We're in the last stretch of the first semester of my senior year. Any explanation will sound like an excuse.

Maybe it started months earlier, this hole that blasted through my chest shortly after my mother left, but it isn't until right then that I feel it filling with a new fear, the fear that Mr. Duvane might actually be right about me. So I pull out my notebook, determined to prove him wrong. I jot down, to me, what sounds like a foreign language. Axons and dendrites. Ionic compounds of cations and anions.

I raise my hand.

Mr. Duvane ignores it. Considering my low test scores, it might not even occur to him to look my way.

Nevertheless I write down everything I hear and plan on looking up the confusing scientific terms in the textbook when I get home.

Toward the end of the period, Mr. Duvane passes out the study guide, a list of one hundred terms that may or may not be on the final. The sound of his orthopedic shoes screeches up the spine worse than nails on a chalkboard as he reaches us in the nosebleed seats. He seems satisfied he has our attention.

"For some of you the final next Friday is your final chance at passing my class."

* * *

My limbs branch out across the entire couch, the television blaring as my father rigs up the slide projector perched on the kitchen table. All I can see is his burnt forehead and his curly hair greased back with Bryl Creem. The slide projector covers up the rest. He's seated at the table. His arm curls protectively around a tumbler of ouzo as if somebody might take it away. If he's drunk, he's a well-focused one. Next to him is a pad of yellow legal paper.

He is not jotting down notes. In between checking out family slides, he's writing my mother a letter, a love letter, the first he's ever written her, so far as I know.

"Look at this one," he says.

This is the third time I've had to turn down *Die Hard*.

I hear the hum of the projector and secretly wish the bulb inside would pop and burn out. Bruce Willis has just launched a terrorist through the window of a skyscraper, the body descending on a squad car, wrecking the hood. This part I've seen before. Over his shoulder, Bruce says, "Welcome to the party, pal."

Reluctantly I get up off the couch. When he gets this way he either laments the loss of my mother or regrets never having cheated on her. "There was that trip to Syracuse," he likes to always bring up. When I think of hot cities in which to have an affair, Syracuse, with its wind chill factor and Canadian cold fronts, isn't the first city that comes to mind. He had been away on business with his client, the late restaurant owner from Bel Air. Women were forever plentiful around that man.

Tonight, however, it's a melancholic slide show down memory lane, Fernwood Street in Lynwood where my parents owned their first home, to be precise.

"Your mother just doesn't get it," my father says. "What man is going to love her when she loses her arms and legs?"

During her pregnancy with my younger brother, my mother developed type II diabetes.

"Dad," I say, rattled by his grim prognosis of my mother's disease. "She takes medication for it."

My father shakes his head and furiously writes as if I've sparked a new line of thought, a new argument the attorney in him hasn't tried out on her yet.

"You're wrong about that, Paula Girl. Pills won't be enough. She'll have to start shooting herself with insulin. Even then, the way she eats sweets, it's only a matter of time before it goes after her limbs."

"You're not telling her that in the letter, are you?"

My father is too busy crossing lines out and writing above them to answer. Part of me is afraid to look. I imagine the horror on her face upon opening his letter at the mailbox. Amputated limbs. Needles and insulin shots. It will probably prove too shocking and she'll rip it up, convinced he's out to hurt her. She won't understand how hard it was for him to write, how hard it is for him to stop loving her.

He shifts to the side so I can look through the lenses at my mother standing on a patch of lawn. Her black hair is pulled into a high ponytail and her hands are folded underneath the swell of her belly that is me. She wears red lipstick and smiles so that the gap in her front teeth shows.

I pull back. My mother is beautiful.

"This was taken in front of my mom's house," my father says. "Before the city forced us out to build the freeway."

When my parents first married, they bought a two bedroom house on the border between Lynwood and Compton. What proved far more dangerous to a young couple just starting out than a neighborhood rampant with late night shootings and stabbings was their proximity to my father's mother. My father loved being so close to his mother and demented Uncle Gil who still lived at home, having dropped out of college after a professor in the psychology department reportedly wanted to float his brain for research. None of the family ever deflated Yia Yia's belief that it was her youngest son's high IQ, not his troubled mind, which made him the perfect subject for such a barbaric sounding test. Yia Yia was a lonely widow living in a bad neighborhood and needed a live-in companion, a protector of sorts. Uncle Gil with his ever growing arsenal of guns and knives and deadly self-defense moves worked better at thwarting off neighbors and criminals alike than any Beware of Dog sign at the side gate or an expensive burglar alarm system.

For obvious reasons, my mother didn't like going over to the house. For one, she wasn't Greek. My mother is a mutt—German, English, Irish, and some Native American, the Kikapu Tribe from her father's side. The Indian part made her especially unpopular in a family full of European immigrants. My late pappou even blamed my other grand-father's alcoholism on living on a reservation with nothing to do but collect welfare checks and get drunk with the cash. He'd ignore my mother's polite reminders that her father was born and raised in a board-ing house the family ran in Slaten, Texas.

The other reason my mother hated coming over for Sunday din-ner was that she'd find herself being sexually grilled in the kitchen by Yia Yia. Slipping her daughter-in-law an index card with the recipe for Spanakopitas rolled in pastry phyllo or Souvlaki, barbecued skewers of roasted lamb, the occasional sexual position would be discreetly written down on the back—from behind, from the side, from the foot of the bed, as if these acts were as practical to learn for a young wife as how to sauté an onion or make your own salad dressing with olive oil and oregano.

"You want to be a whore in the bedroom and a chef in the kitchen, honey."

My mother soon learned it was easier to just thank the woman, then rip up the explicit directions later once my mother was home. During the meal Uncle Gil stared too much and complimented my mother on everything from the dainty way she chewed her food to the shade of her lipstick.

"Did you get a good look?" my father asks. He sounds impatient, like he wants to move on.

I nod. The slides seem to energize him, and I'd rather see him this way, obsessed with how things used to be, than despondent over how they are now. It occurs to me that this might be a good time to ask him about something I know he doesn't want to discuss.

"Have you talked to that man?"

"What man?"

"Jesus, Dad," I say. "The one who gets off on taking pictures of underage girls." This gets my father's attention, this gets him to actually hear me.

"When did he fucking do that?"

"The other morning on my way to school."

My father appears pulled between our nasty situation and the tunnel of memories seen only through the lenses right before his eyes. He clicks the button and makes me see what he does. It's a picture of me as a little girl, maybe four, with a ribbon of pink yarn in my curly dark hair. Pink seems like such an obvious feminine color and I resent my mother for dressing me like my older sister, the little girl's girl she hoped I'd become. I'm on a tricycle and pushing the pedals with patent leather shoes. One of my feet is blurry from slipping off the pedal and my face is red and a size too big, my mouth held in mid-cry. Clearly, I'm miserable.

"Don't worry about that *poutsos*," my father finally says. "He's just a former client. I'll take care of it."

But I don't believe him.

"How?"

"That isn't for you to goddamn know." My father is defensive, fighting the only person who is on his side, and when he looks up at me I'm expecting him to scold and curse at me more. Instead he leans back a little, and points to the projector. "Your mother took this picture. It's when you first learned how to ride a bike. No training wheels. No nothing. Do you remember?"

I shake my head and glance over at the TV. Barefoot and bloodied, Bruce is running across broken glass. The death toll is up to three.

"You can't see me," my father says. "I'm running alongside you on the grass."

I bend down and pair my eyes to the lenses, though I see something different, and it's hard not to pity him for being so blind as to how things changed between them after my sister and I were born. In my mother's eyes her children came first. Slowly or quickly, at some point my father faded into the background of her life. Even thirteen years before she walked out on him, I see how easily it was for her to eliminate him from the picture.

CLOSING ARGUMENTS

As luck would have it my father meant what he said about getting the ex-husband to back off because for the next week and a half there are no midnight games of horseshoe, no early morning drive by's. During this time I cram for the Chemistry final. Flashcards with the term on one side and the definition on the back are strewn about the house. At every opportunity, I quiz myself—while drying my hair in the bathroom or toasting a pair of frozen waffles in the kitchen.

I recite the definitions for ions, electrons, and ionic compounds until I know them cold. Atoms with an electric charge. Negative electricity in an atom. A chemical compound held together by ionic bonds in a lattice structure. I even draw a little ladder as an illustration.

On the morning of the final, I don't wait by my car for Trevor to find me and walk me to class the way he's been doing now for the past few days. Instead I'm nearly five minutes early to class, a sharpened number two pencil and a Scantron in hand. Mr. Duvane doesn't notice because he isn't even in the room. So I take this last chance to flash through my cards and go over the terms.

It isn't until well after the tardy bell that he arrives, looking disheveled, looking more grave than drunk. In his arms are a messy stack of papers fresh from the Xerox machine because they still carry that copy smell.

"Yesterday, someone broke into my desk and stole the answer key for the final."

Lucia stretches off to the side, my side.

"He probably just got wasted and misplaced it," she whispers.

Mr. Duvane drops a pile of tests on the front desk of each row. He won't look at any of us, not even Kimberly Foley who quickly takes one of the tests and passes the rest over her shoulder.

When I receive my test copy, I recognize nothing on it. There are no scientific terms, only formulas.

I throw up my hand and call out before he calls on me.

"This is the pretest for Physics."

Mr. Duvane casts a suspicious glance like I'm the one who stole his answer key since my entire class grade rides on passing this test.

"Yes, Paula. That's exactly what it is."

"But you haven't covered any of this."

"Whoever stole my final has penalized the entire class, including you."

Panic rises up in me with nowhere to put it, nowhere to hide from the certainty that the one hundred terms from the study guide I know back to front are now meaningless. Before I even pick up my pencil and fill in the first bubble on the Scantron, I already know I've failed.

* * *

Right after lunch I head thankfully to the attendance office to check out. At this point even a shrink's office with month old *Newsweek* magazines and a fish tank filled with exotic carp are a reprieve from obsessing over blowing Mr. Duvane's pretest/final. My father's secretary is supposed to have called the school, pretending to be my mother.

On my way, I spot Trevor breaking away from his crowd of friends. Becky is with him, and he's taking it nice and slow after the bell, the way he's walked with me a couple mornings now, making me late to Chemistry. His fingers loosely hook into hers with the kind of ease that suggests they've been hooking up in even closer ways.

I hope I'm around the corner in time before he sees that I see, before I see him kiss her.

The woman working at the attendance window is chomping on a celery stick smothered in peanut butter. Her mouth full, she points with the stringy part toward the nearby bench. She wants me to take a seat while she processes my pass.

But when I turn around, I find Trevor waiting for me.

"What are you doing out here, ditcher."

He's in a good mood, which, because of who I just saw him with, automatically puts me in a bad one.

Telling him I have an appointment with a psychiatrist will make me sound like the head trip that I am—the sad girl who sits in the back, with the failing grades who has to leave school early because her mother has left her with abandonment issues. I may as well paint my fingernails black and wear hard rock t-shirts.

I walk clear around Trevor on my way to the bench, hoping to avoid her smell on him. All the cheerleaders wear the same pink colored scent designed for girl's half their age—Love's Baby Soft.

"I have to go to the dentist."

"Sure you do." Trevor sits too close, leaning forward to catch a side glance of my leg.

This is Southern California and even in late fall, after the morning fog burns off, it's warm enough for shorts and flip flops. I worry if I shaved.

"Who'd you get to call for you," he asks, "your college boyfriend?" It seems like he's only half-joking.

Now that I see he's full on jealous, I decide to play along. "He's a little older," I say. "Probably around your dad's age."

This gets him laughing. Instead of slapping his own knee, he slips his hand on mine. A move so fast, I have no time to stop it.

"He'd like you. My dad loves his young brunettes."

The way he says this tells me his parents are either divorced or should be.

Slowly, Trevor's hand makes its way up my thigh.

It's his throwing hand he's touching me with and although I like feeling the rough places on his palm where he's pitched and held things the hardest, I start to pull away. I'm afraid how far he's willing to take this.

"It's okay," he says. He stops at the fabric and fingers the hem of my shorts.

Just then the partition slides all the way up.

"Your pass is ready."

Trevor winks at the woman.

"Give us a second. She's telling me a secret."

She isn't sure how to respond and leaves my pass outside the window, held down by a stapler so it won't fly away.

Trevor turns back to me. "I like you, but everybody wants me to be with Becky."

In a way the words are expected, which somehow takes me even more by surprise. I let myself be misled. Just five minutes before, he was making out with her. I *saw* him kissing her. As I try and get up Trevor takes a firmer hold of my leg. I imagine his red prints on my skin.

"Let me finish." He leans closer, and I smell the corn chips he had for lunch, his spicy hot Fritos breath. "You interest me," he says again as if I missed the best part. "So I want to see you on the side."

At seventeen I know what he says isn't right. As I write this, though, being a woman who has heard her share of come on lines, what I remember most about what he said is that it sounded at once, too straightforward, too deceitful. They were the words of a man, not a boy.

* * *

I park on the street in front of my father's office because I don't plan to stay long. All I need is twenty bucks for gas and a drive-thru dinner at Jack-in-the-Box.

From outside I hear shouting, the kind that brings men to blows. As I open the door, I recognize it's my father and another man—the ex-husband is back. Nora is nowhere to be found and must still be at lunch.

Uncomfortably, I take a seat on the couch. I don't need to eavesdrop since I can hear everything loud and clear from the reception area. I think about waiting in the car. I think about calling the cops.

"You won't get away with robbing her blind," the man says. "I'll have you disbarred."

"You're the fucking thief," my father fires back.

His voice is thunderous, yet controlled. "This is about my finding all that property you tried hiding from her." Like a good defense attorney, he counts a calculated beat for effect. "Did you really think I wouldn't know where to look?"

In a strange way, I'm proud. Even if my father is as guilty as her ex-husband of stealing her money, it's been months since I've seen him take a swing at anything, let alone the ex who's been harassing us for weeks.

My father isn't finished with him yet. I hear an ominous rustling sound, like he might have the man by the shirt, maybe by the throat. Whatever my father says next he can't risk another person hearing, and I think of the red eye home from Hawaii, how he said he'd never let anyone come near me or Rhea. He's making up for more than somebody's camera happy ex-husband who snapped my picture. He's making up for having ignored in his younger brother what he'd so obviously seen in the pedophiles he's defended. Their excuses as flimsy as a groin pull in the backseat of a car or steadfast in the denial like the local congressman who passed a lie detector test with flying colors after having been caught literally red handed, jerking off behind a dumpster at a local park.

Maybe what happened to my sister and me was payback for their sentences being reduced or thrown out altogether because she was seventeen, not sixteen, because the children out playing didn't really see the man all that clearly and the woman who did was well into her sixties, wore prescription sunglasses, and clearly needed to have her eyes checked again. The politician, in his suit and tie, could've been rooting through garbage as he claims, looking for cans to recycle. He campaigned on cleaning up the environment, after all.

I'm contemplating heading into the room and breaking it up before my father needs a lawyer himself, when the decision is made for me. By fear or by rage, in the ex-husband's haste to leave, he flashes past without even a glance at me seated picture perfect on the couch.

Minutes later we're on the 60 freeway in my father's Mercedes. He cancels the rest of his afternoon and insists on driving me to Studio City, to see the shrink. Afterward he promises we'll wait out the traffic at Jerry's Famous Deli and split a foot long hoagie.

The air conditioning blows hard and cold, and somewhere between Pasadena and Burbank, I tell my father about flunking Mr. Duvane's final.

He smiles and shakes his head as if I've told him a joke that isn't all that funny.

"So you retake the class. Big deal."

After my father blew his knee his senior year at high school, he lost his free ride to play guard at Stanford. So he attended UCLA for his Bachelor's Degree instead. He finished his Master's in Business in one year instead of two. Then right afterward, he earned his law degree at USC. All before he turned twenty-seven. I know all this because my mother used to tell me. My yia yia brags about it too. He's a legend in this family where his own father, in order to help pay for his sons to attend college, sold fruit out of the flatbed of his pick-up and his mother took in the neighbor's ironing.

Besides, I know better. I know failing a class in my senior year is a big deal and what he's accomplished by this pep talk is damage control.

"I only have one more semester before I graduate. I'll have to go to night school."

"So you'll go to night school."

I think of what Mr. Duvane said about me, how I'll need to get married after I graduate, how my only worth is in my looks. How I don't even have that since Trevor readily admits wanting to keep a girl like me hidden away from the rest of his life. The hole in my chest seems like it's filling up again. I've never cried in front of my father, and I take a couple of deep breaths to keep from starting now.

"I'm a loser, Dad," I blurt out. "There's no way I'll get into a four-year school."

My father swerves into the emergency lane and kills the engine. Cars move their fastest in the lane next to us and the glass of the side window trembles at their speed. It's clear he could care less about the danger. He looks angrier at me now than he did at the man who's threatening to have him disbarred.

"You have no idea how strong you are. Look at what you've survived. Not many girls your age have their mothers leave. And you stayed." That part always gets him, the fact I'm the only one in the family who didn't abandon him. He starts up the car again and looks ahead as if he must.

"You'll retake that class in adult school. You'll earn your diploma in June. Your mother and I will call a truce and watch you receive it from way up in the stands. You'll attend a community college and you'll transfer to the four year of your choice."

When it looks clear, my father guns the gas, and we merge in with the flow of traffic.

"But you won't stop there. You'll earn your Master's. Then you'll shove your degree in that *psoli's* face and show him you now hold one higher than his."

I fight not to smile at his ranting monologue in my defense. My father is an expert at closing arguments.

STUN

During my third semester at a community college Uncle Dimitri makes amends with my father and me behind Yia Yia and his brother's back. After his wife threw him out of their home for having fronted the tuition for his former mistress to attend the Fashion and Art Institute in L.A., what heart he had left inevitably failed him. He needs someplace far removed from his own to recover from the subsequent surgery. To pay him back, Aunt Lorna had waited until he won big on an exacta at Hollywood Park and deposited the winnings in their joint account. Then she promptly served him with divorce papers in her brand new fully loaded, fully paid for Porsche 911.

He also needs my father's help in preparing for an upcoming trial, a shocking sexual assault case involving a man, his ex-girlfriend, and a stun gun. Seeking thirty plus years for felony kidnapping and assault for something so perverse it's made the papers and the local news, the D.A.'s office is in no mood to settle for anything less. As a criminal lawyer, Uncle Dimitri rarely steps foot inside a courtroom. The majority of his cases are plea deals, reached under the table at an expensive lunch on his dime with prosecutors or out on the green with judges, playing eighteen holes, letting them win.

On the morning Uncle Dimitri is to be released from the hospital, he waits in a chair, not in his bed, wearing a track suit and new white tennis shoes that look like this is the first they've ever touched the ground. In the seven years I haven't seen him, he's lost more hair, more weight. My father says his four sons visited but there is no sign of them now, no flowers or get well cards. I have come with my boyfriend, Erick, while my father impatiently circles the parking lot.

"You're gorgeous, honey," Uncle Dimitri says like he says to all women. He shakes his head, smiling. "Thank Christ you look nothing like your father." But we both know I look everything like him and my father looks everything like his, which is where the jab comes from. Uncle Dimitri has always been a little sore that he took after his prematurely aged mother—the yearly rise in more forehead, the deep-set dark eyes. I lean down so he can kiss my cheek, and just below the zipper of his jacket his chest is stained not with blood but with iodine, used to keep the incision clean after surgery.

I introduce him to my boyfriend Erick and Uncle Dimitri sizes him up too soon. Short. Pale. Long hair. Quiet. He is no Greek.

Uncle Dimitri isn't impressed and tells Erick to wait like a child, like a nuisance, in the room while he takes me over to the one next door and introduces me to a fellow patient, the big and bald Telly Savalas and his entourage of fellow Greeks. If Erick is offended, it isn't in his nature to voice it. He's in a grunge band called The Chronic Cult and writes his own lyrics, including an embarrassing ballad about me called "Picturing Paula," comparing my big brown eyes to tiny TV screens, both sets apparently addictive to watch. In a few weeks they're playing a gig, their biggest yet, at Bogart's, a club in Long Beach, with an actual marquee out front and a mosh pit inside for fans to bodily collide or sway in slow unison, gripping cigarette lighters above their heads.

Telly Savalas used to play a New York City cop on TV who somehow pulled off looking tough busting criminals while sucking on a trademark lollipop. After I tell him about the catch phrase "kickback Kojack" we used in high school whenever somebody was too nosy, he insists on autographing a coffee stained paper napkin I don't ask for. Celebrities are nothing new for Uncle Dimitri considering he used to live in Toluca Lake, the town right next to the TV and movie studios in Burbank.

Only when he is wheeled out curbside and scrunches up his face at the wheels that will take him all the way to Chino, a hay truck idling in the red, do I see my yia yia in him. My father must see his reaction too because water squirts out at the windshield and the wipers smear, not clear, the dirt that's collected on the glass from being parked in the backyard. Obviously this is a step down for Uncle Dimitri even though he specifically requested a vehicle he would have to climb up in since he can't bend over so well.

"Jesus, Paul," Uncle Dimitri says, struggling out of the chair, struggling not to laugh because the staples have just come out and it hurts too much. "At the very least you could've driven my luxury limo through a set of sprinklers on your way over."

* * *

Having his tougher older brother in the house balances my father in a way I haven't been able to. Unlike Psycho Gil, who needs full armor and artillery, Uncle Dimitri has no understanding of physical weakness and actually tried to walk off his heart attack while it was happening. For a couple of hours he was successful at it, meeting all of his court appearances that afternoon before the throb in his arm thrust through other parts, through organs and bone, blurring his vision and seizing his stomach. He collapsed on the floor in his office where his assistant called the paramedics. Tests showed he needed a quadruple bypass. "A blocked artery for every pack a day I smoked," Uncle Dimitri likes to joke.

My father needs the money Uncle Dimitri is going to split with him from the trial. The financial upkeep off his investments proves too much. The other night, before Uncle Dimitri came to stay, we ate dinner by lantern light because he remembered to pay the hefty monthly stable fees for his fleet of Walking Horses yet neglected to take care of the seventy five dollar past due electric bill. Twice I've had to pull off a neon orange warning taped to the front door notifying us that our home will be auctioned if the mortgage payments are not up to date by the end of the month. The ex-husband is still after him too, having lodged a formal complaint with the State Bar. But my father isn't as concerned as he should be. "You know how bogged down they are with clients throwing a tantrum in the goddamn sandbox about us no good shysters? We're always doing something wrong," he said, laughing. "Winning too much. Not winning enough. Relax, Paula Girl. It'll take years before they ever get to that *poutsos'* fairytale allegations."

With Uncle Dimitri here I no longer have to worry about other things, nightly things, like my father and his Savage, his putting down too many bottles of ouzo, his relentless need to relive a life that is no longer his through a projector and slides. I no longer have to rattle my door knob before coming out of my room, pretending not to see him on the couch retracting his hand out of his sweatpants and changing the Playboy Channel.

*   *   *

While my father is researching cases on kidnappings and sexual assault at the law library, I drive Uncle Dimitri to the corner of Foothill Boulevard and Haven Avenue in the upper middle-class community of Rancho Cucamonga where it all started, where the woman apparently flagged down her ex. Although Uncle Dimitri is getting around better, he doesn't feel up to driving.

After she came out of the bank, her car wouldn't start. Her ex just happened to be driving by. For some reason this raised in her no red flags. He offered her a ride back to her place but took her to his instead. In the driveway is where the prosecutors claim the kidnapping began. He dragged her inside. He tied her to a chair. For three days in the same room where they'd made love, he electrocuted, he burned her breasts and between her thighs at whim until somehow she was able to get away, diving head first through the bathroom window. Six stitches in her forehead. Lacerations across the palms of her hands. Palpable but not significant damage to the breasts and genital area. The clinical way my uncle and father discuss her injuries is enough to excuse me from the table, enough for me to cover up the graphic photos with a magazine or a book whenever I see them left lying out.

"The cuts could've been self-inflicted," Uncle Dimitri poses when I bring up her injuries. "Six stitches is kid's stuff. She could've hurt herself on purpose. Nobody was in that bathroom with her. Or she could've been coming off a bad drug trip and didn't realize she could leave through the front door."

"Does she have a history of drug use?"

Uncle Dimitri shrugs.

"Does it matter? All it takes is for me to put it out there."

From his coat pocket he pulls out a ticking stopwatch. "Make a right at the next light," he says. We're timing the trip, scrutinizing every second for possible discrepancies in the testimony she gave at the pretrial hearing.

"They had that kind of relationship," he insists.

"Break up, get back together. Break up again. Several 911 calls. 'He slapped me. She kicked me in the balls.' God knows how many times the cops came out to find one of them saying it was just a disagreement that got out of hand. From what he tells me, she's no innocent. Those two were into some kinky shit."

"I'd hardly call a stun gun a sex toy."

"Okay," Uncle Dimitri concedes. "We're kind of fucked there."

Part of me regrets coming even if I do get to spend time with Uncle Dimitri. I am to play the woman, the victim who bears in the most personal places the physical scars of over seventy-two hours of torture from the man she used to love, the man she trusted enough to give her a ride to her home. I am supposed to retrace her steps, pretend to be tied to the same chair, wriggle my chest, my pelvis, and legs, through the same shattered window.

The Peter Tasakas rape case happened on a sunny morning like this, only on a residential street. Darkly good looking. Suit and tie. Audi. He had all the makings of the kind of guy you'd give your phone number to, maybe even get in the front seat of his car to flirt, just flirt. Both men must've known they were clear to attack. No woman is expecting danger in broad daylight. That was how Erick and I met—idling in our cars during rush hour traffic, side door to side door, on the 57 freeway. For miles, inching past exit after exit, our eyes were on each other, on our opportunities that were slowly passing us by, until finally he exclaimed, "Okay, okay, you win. I can't take it anymore. Please, pull over!"

Uncle Dimitri knows his way around a neighborhood he's never been in. His client told him the way. When we arrive at a condominium complex made of stucco, the roof of terra cotta tile, he knows the combination for the gate to let us in. He clicks off his stopwatch.

"How long?" I ask.

"Nearly three minutes. She said a little over two."

Good. Her testimony withstands the test of time.

Part of me wants her to be telling the truth. At the front door of his client's condo, he has me get the key from under the welcome mat. He uses it to break the police tape and we let ourselves inside.

Nothing is out of place, which is somehow sinister in and of itself. But he's an accountant by trade who tidies up numbers all day. A clean house only makes sense. The kitchen is immaculate, the counter wiped down. No dishes in the sink.

A picture of a man is on top of the entertainment center. He's scrawny and pasty in a pair of swimming trunks, plastic visor and one dopey grin. A t-shirt covers his chest to protect him from the sun or from the scrutiny of other beach goers. His ex-girlfriend is with him in a bikini, her chest flat, her brown hair teased big. Neither one of them is particularly attractive. They are about the same height, the same frame. It's obvious how their fights became volatile. Just above her breast, she has an unmistakable bruise, the size of a silver dollar.

"What's the name of that little rocker you're seeing?" Uncle Dimitri asks.

"Erick," I say insulted at how a picture of his sex fiend client reminds him of my boyfriend.

"I shouldn't be telling you this, but I don't want you getting hurt by a man like me. Make no mistake, they're all like me." Uncle Dimitri takes the picture off my hands of the couple during happier times before things turned, before the police, lawyers and the State of California barged into their relationship with handcuffs and court orders, before they became the prosecution's star witness and the defendant standing to do serious prison time. "He may not act like it, but he's one arrogant little prick," Uncle Dimitri says. "Don't let him fool you. It's none of my business if you're having sex with him, but you make damn sure you beat his ass to the door afterward. That way you'll always have the upper hand." Uncle Dimitri zips up the picture in his jacket to discard later—possible evidence the cops have now lost since they didn't think to bag it on the first round.

* * *

The trial lasts for less than two weeks and my father and Uncle Dimitri exploit the coverage, talking to the press enough times for my father to clip the articles and blot out the entire freezer door of the fridge like a kid with A papers.

Every night at Yanni's restaurant over flaming cheese and stuffed vine leaves for appetizers, lemony Avgolemono soup and moussaka, flaky and meaty, for the main course, Uncle Dimitri and my father give me a rundown of what happened in court. I cancel two dinners in one week with Erick. He says he understands. He needs the extra time to practice for the band's big gig at Bogart's.

"The prosecution lost points today," my father says, switching from ouzo to coffee. He needs a clear head for court tomorrow and cuts himself off right after dinner.

"The D.A. should know better than to bore a jury with facts. Who cares if there were rope burns found on her wrists. She already admitted to having rough sex with him in the past."

Uncle Dimitri laughs, digging into his pocket for another toothpick to contend with the craving for an after meal smoke.

"I can't read that little fucker in the back."

My father crosses his arms across his belly that's getting bigger and bigger every year without my mother.

"We've got an ace in the hole with that *poutsaki*."

Uncle Dimitri nods and it's as if I've missed something.

"That reminds me, Paula. We need you at closing arguments on Friday."

"Why me?" I ask my father.

"Moral support," he explains. "Besides, you've never seen the Priamos brothers in action."

Uncle Dimitri pulls out his wallet to cover the check.

"For putting up with us," he says offering me up two C-notes, and I feel like I am being paid for services yet to be rendered.

* * *

The prosecutor is a woman in her fifties, seasoned at the job and talks freely, assuredly to the jury, without benefit of notes. "This isn't a case of domestic abuse or even experimental sex as the defense would like to lead you to believe. What happened to the victim in this case is sadistic and cruel."

In the box the jurors watch her intently and an Asian woman in the front is writing something down. At about this time my father, who sits at the defendant's table with his arms folded at his chest, drops his head, nodding off.

The judge notices. He frowns, but says nothing. If he does, if he reprimands my father it will only draw attention to what my father wants the jury to see—the prosecution's closing argument is boring him to sleep.

And if the jurors aren't catching my father catching some Z's, then there's Uncle Dimitri to look at, who is up out of his chair and is motioning for me to meet him at the waist length gate that separates the players from the spectators.

"Paula," he says. He's close enough for me to know he's drunk entirely too much coffee today. "I need you to go downstairs to the lobby and buy me some spearmint gum."

Gum? He's just gotten up in the middle of the prosecution's closing argument, the prime time for him to throw her off rhythm with random objections, to have me buy him gum? No. There's another reason for this and that's when I see "the little fucker in the back," the guy with the neatly trimmed hair, wearing a Cal Poly sweatshirt. He's around my age. He's checking me out in the bright white dress I bought with the money Uncle Dimitri gave me at dinner. He's putting it together that I'm working somehow with my Uncle, that I'm for the defense. I'm for the weak kneed accountant who gets a sick sexual charge off electricity, who sits in an expensive suit, between his two intimidating Greek lawyers that will stop at nothing to win, not even if it means pimping out to the courtroom their own flesh and blood.

Their case could ride on something this innocuous, this small, so to please my father and uncle, I return the juror's stare, my smile worth every dollar.

My father may have opened the trial with all the grunt work he's done, similar cases of this vs. that, which were thrown up as a means of deflection, as tangible outside evidence the jurors could grasp onto if they didn't want to find the defendant guilty. But Uncle Dimitri does all the arguing, the charming, the inoffensive jokes with the jurors. He seduces them all the way he seduces so many women, including the Asian woman in front who is no longer taking notes. She can't take her eyes off him, his mouth with all those easy words coming out, that's hiding a stick of Juicy Fruit in the back.

He makes no mention of the stun gun. Instead he reminds the jury of the unorthodox relationship the defendant and victim shared, the explosiveness on both sides, the three times the police had been called.

Most defense attorneys know the less time they stand before the jury, the more time it will seem the prosecutors spend trying to prove their case. And with Uncle Dimitri, he takes twenty minutes and when he's finished he points at my father who has been wide awake this whole time, his arm stretched across the defendant's chair. Uncle Dimitri says right on cue, "A certain member of the defense may've been caught resting when he shouldn't have been, but let me reassure you, the jury, that both members of the defense humbly rest before you now."

While the jury is deliberating, my father calls the office and Uncle Dimitri takes me on a walk. He points out a stunning blond in spiked heels, a woman who looks more like she should be rolling around sexily on a Jaguar in a hard rock music video than standing outside a court-house having a smoke.

"You see her, Paula? She's a prison groupie. Only the knockouts go after the real animals." He says this like he's somewhere between disgusted and envious.

Fifty-five minutes later, after the jury returns and the verdicts are read, this woman will cry out from deep in the gallery that they have found the love of her life guilty of sexual assault, the felony kidnapping charges dropped in some kind of bizarre compromise amongst its members. Her cry will be real but it will not be out of despair. It will be out of all that lies ahead of her. The prison visits. The collect phone calls. All that letter writing. A violent man under her control, who will have no other choice but to hold onto her every word because he's not allowed to ever hold onto her.

* * *

That night when my father and uncle want to celebrate the kidnapping charge being dropped, I have to pass because it's Erick and the band's first gig at Bogart's. With my uncle staying at the house and the trial, I haven't been spending as much time as I should with Erick and I want to make it up to him. He sneaks me in the back entrance because I'll be turned away if I try legally through the front. There isn't time to change and I'm in the bright white dress and red suede flats I wore earlier at the trial.

The air inside is loaded with smoke — cigarette, clove, especially marijuana that anybody could get high off just by breathing it second-hand. From coming to these clubs I know each drug's distinctive smell, but I've never tried cloves or pot. On the first night I hung out with Erick and his band members and their girlfriends, I made a lasting impression when somebody passed around a bong and instead of taking a hit, I excused myself and sat on the fire escape steps. Erick said he was interested in me even more after that. I could think for myself. More like I was petrified by my father who said if I ever was arrested for drugs or a D.U.I. I would regret him coming to get me. He has his reasons. During a drug deal gone bad, a client's cute twenty-two year old son was stabbed in the lung while seated at the wheel of his car, the engine still running. It happened in the parking lot of a convenience store in Lynwood. With the knife still in his chest, the guy drove himself to the same hospital where my sister and I were born.

I sit with all the other girlfriends. One has peroxide white hair, the others have dyed theirs black. All of them are in black dresses, black nail polish. Their faces are a shade paler with carefully traced blood red lips because it's contrast they're after.

"You'll have to excuse what I'm wearing," I say. "I didn't have time to change."

Lisa, the one with the peroxide hair, smiles slowly. She's high. She's the lead singer's girl and instead of car keys and a wallet full of cash in her purse, she keeps a bent spoon and a baggie of heroin to burn.

"You look cute," she says.

"I look like a nightlight."

The black haired girls laugh a little too hard. We're friendly with each other because we have to be.

Soon after The Chronic Cult takes to the stage the crowd takes to their music, reacting loud enough between sets for the band to be invited back. The lead singer is dark skinned with a dark beard and reminds me of a Lakers player except he's druggie thin. Practically every lyric to every song is screamed, not sung. I've grown used to cheering on music I can't understand. I cheer extra hard during Eric's solo as he slouches with the weight of his guitar, showing off his finger work. By their last set, a daiquiri shows up in front of me, including a juicy strawberry pierced into the lip of the glass.

Compliments of a hot long haired guy, all leather and nose rings, whose presence alone at our table snatches every girlfriend's attention off the stage and on him. He crouches next to me. He smells musky like patchouli oil.

"Something to match those sweet shoes," he says to me.

I'm not sure what to make of his pick-up line. Either the guy has a foot fetish or he's making fun of me, maybe both. In my get up, I can't exactly blame him. I thank him for the drink, for the alcohol I can't buy for myself. He leaves but I'm concerned he'll be back. The girlfriends tell me he's Jungle George, the headliner of the club, a guy who has not only slept with and dumped most every girl in here but most recently dumped his own band when he was offered a record deal.

He returns with another daiquiri while Erick and the rest get off stage, while I'm sucking up the last of the first one he gave me.

"I want to have sex with you," he says.

His straightforwardness is refreshing, repulsive.

"Erick, the guitarist," I say like he doesn't already know. "He's my boyfriend."

"Really?" Jungle George sounds a little skeptical and even more sarcastic. "I don't think you're his type anymore. Look for yourself."

Erick is chatting at the side of the stage with the girl who sings folksy songs. She played before The Chronic Cult with nothing but a barstool to sit on and an acoustic guitar in her lap. She's in a shapeless dress, Birkenstock sandals, make-up less. Whatever she's telling him, he looks flattered. He smiles. I see his hand throw back his long hair, the fingernails on the right hand he keeps long so he can better manipulate the strings. He's flirting like a girl.

I feel the blow of his effeminate gesture. Then I feel nothing. Erick's guitar is left open in its case and I go over and buckle it closed. Together they weigh roughly an entire bale of hay, but anger knows no weakness and I carry it off with little effort. I carry it right out the exit door.

In the parking lot a few seconds later I predictably hear my name ricocheting off the buildings. Taking his instrument was the only way to steal his attention away from Flabby Miss Folk Lore.

"Where are you going with that?"

"To the pawn store to hock this piece of crap. What do you think I could get for it? Fifty bucks?"

"Why are you being such a bitch?" Erick follows my lead down the back steps of the club, down into the insults and name calling. "You think you can just show up to one of my gigs and pretend like you haven't been blowing me off?"

I stop in the middle of the parking lot, Erick at the curb.

I'm jealous and angry at him for humiliating me in front of a guy who got his stage name from the muscle bound cartoon character who wears a loin cloth and swings from vine to vine. I'm angry and humiliated with myself for allowing my own father and uncle to use me as a bit player in their courtroom theatrics that have nothing to do with fairness or the rule of law.

"Don't try and turn things around," I shout at Erick. "I don't work that way."

"You're impossible to get close to, Paula. You know that? You do everything your old man says." He runs his hand through his hair fitfully, not casually like he had with the folk girl. "What'd he tell you to do? Start a fight so you can have an excuse to walk away?" This is not how I planned things. Erick's voice isn't supposed to be louder than mine. He's supposed to back down. He's supposed to apologize for not noticing the headliner of the club hitting on me. "Go ahead," he yells. "Go home to him. Leave. There's no room in your heart for anybody else anyway."

I set the guitar down, left with very little options. Erick's right about me and this does nothing except make me hate him for pointing it out. There's still time for me to meet him halfway. For me to say I'm sorry. I love you. We could take it back to Erick's apartment not far from here in Belmont Shore and work that hot tension from our fight for all its worth. We could laugh about it later the next morning after we've woken up still in each other's arms. He could scramble me eggs with tarragon and I could return with two mucho grande cups of coffee from Juan Java's. But the folk lore girl is in between us, in one way or another, and I remember what Uncle Dimitri said about him, about all men. My car is only a couple lengths away and with the distance I have on him, I can easily get to the door first.

WHAT THEY TOLD ME AFTER HE DIED

I am sorry you lost your father. But look at it this way. At least by hooking up with my husband, you've gained a *father figure*.

—Holly Brown, Jim Brown's ex-wife

Sugar never hung with a bad crowd. So what if she went home with a customer now and then. I wouldn't read much into that. She wasn't no hooker. She has a jealous ex who won't leave her alone. You talk to him yet?

—Erica

Your father wouldn't stop taking money that wasn't his. Horses, the house, properties. Whatever settlements he got for his clients, he felt like they were partly his too. I warned you. Didn't I warn you?

—June Priamos

I may have my share of problems, but I love you and I can promise you one thing—nobody in that fucked up family of yours will *ever* hurt you again.

—Jim Brown

He used to tell me he loved me too. Right before he damn near knocked the wind out of me with one of his bear hugs.

—Nick Priamos

He just stopped paying for 'em. One day he was king of the industry, next day I owned his prized motherfuckin' high stepper. Hey, how's your sister doin'?

—Fletcher Wilson, horse trainer.

You can't blame Sugar for that brother coming out of the bushes with a gun. Hell, Honey, it's Compton. What did he expect?

—Erica

In high school he picked fights for fun. He'd run his mouth off in the last seconds of a game. Sometimes I'd have to jump in and back him up. He loved to fight, the smell of someone else's blood on his hands. Why do you think he became a defense lawyer? Of course he flipped off that low life fucker who pulled a gun on him. I'm surprised that's all he did.

—Uncle Dimitri

STRUCK

Halfway inside the crosswalk I'm suddenly lifted onto the hood of a pale blue hatchback. Through the windshield the driver and I meet eyes—me with my face pressed up against the glass, her white knuckling the wheel. Her mouth is an open scream. Maybe mine is too. What strikes me first, even before the pain, is that I might die. If the impact hasn't killed me, then it will be when she finally comes to her senses and puts on the brakes.

And she does. As I'm driven into the air, I scramble for a plan, throwing my arms behind me in an attempt to cushion my fall. My landing is a success. I'm still breathing. Sprawled on the asphalt is when the pain hits everywhere and nowhere except in my leg. The throb and pull is so bone deep I'm convinced if I look I may find that it's ripped off at the knee, my calf and foot in its thick-lipped running shoe flung like litter in the middle of the street. On the weekends I jog this route down Walnut Avenue, out of the city and into dairy land. Ever since my father lost the house, I rent a room from an old Portuguese lady, a friend of Lucia's mother. By not paying the mortgages on our house, my father has found a way for my mother to keep hers. In her pasture grazes my trail horse Boo Boo. She may as well have taken Pierre too, because not long after I moved, I couldn't wake him one morning in my new room. As for school, though I no longer live with him, my father continued to claim me as a dependant on tax returns he's delinquent in paying. Only after I turned twenty-three did this change, and I am considered free of him by the government, free to attend a four year university full-time on financial aid and scholarships.

How it stands now, getting up off the road is more crucial to me than if I'll make it to classes on Monday. On one side of the street are tract homes, the other a field full of black and white cows standing on hills of their own fertilizer. The woman gets out of her car. She's stout, dark, and in cold blue hospital scrubs. She reminds me of a Samoan. Her hands are on her hips.

"What should I do?" she asks me.

Given what she has on, I find it hard to believe she hasn't a clue.

"Call 911, you idiot," I finally say. I'm shocked at the sound of my own voice, that I'm not cursing at her. Maybe it's because I know I need her help.

Briefly, she glances back at her car, at the open driver's side door. And I know what she's thinking. She's thinking of getting back in. She's thinking of driving around the mess she's made. She's thinking of leaving me here.

Across the street a middle-aged man in a pick-up has stopped too. There's no telling how much he's seen. He's quick in covering me with a scratchy blanket stitched with fox tails. He smells familiar, like horses, and I want him to look at me. I want him to tell me I'm going to be okay. But there are no reassurances, only orders.

"We need to move her," he says to the Samoan. "I used the radio in my truck to call for help."

Before I have a chance to point out that dragging my lame body anywhere isn't the smartest idea, considering I could be bleeding on the inside, they each have me under my arms.

In her statement to the cops, the Samoan claims I ran into the side of her car on purpose. My bare legs marked up by her front bumper tell a different story, which is a relief since I'm unable to speak for myself. An oxygen mask gets placed over my mouth, shoving in air. Paramedics strap my body onto a collapsible gurney, my neck fitted with a brace in case I have more broken bones other than the one in my leg. I know it's broken. I can't feel my foot. I can't move it either. As her car is being fastened onto a tow truck to be impounded, I find some satisfaction in seeing that my knee has taken out one of her headlights.

* * *

My father has never told me he loves me, and if I ever doubt he did, I remember that moment when he parted the curtain to the emergency room stall and looked at me with his good eye. Earlier this year when Beth Anne's ex- husband won his near decade long battle in petitioning for a hearing to have my father disbarred, my father's blood pressure rocketed and blew the vessels in his eyes. For the past three and a half months a pirate's patch has covered the bad one because he doesn't have the money to pay for the procedure to see out of both.

Medical insurance was one of the first things to go. Pending the out-come of the State Bar's hearing, all of his assets and bank accounts were frozen except for the apple and almond groves in San Joaquin Valley he owns with his former client and current roommate, Rex O'Dell. For now, those investments are in Rex's name. Rex used to be a Hell's Angel until a rocky bout with schizophrenia, the real kind unlike Bared's convenient diagnosis, ended his road trips, leaving him tripping in another way, holed up in an exclusive gated community in Anaheim Hills. Proof of Rex's old freewheeling lifestyle, a beautiful chopped Harley full of chrome is parked like a showpiece in his living room. On probation for having run a casino out of the upstairs bedrooms, equipped with slots and black jack tables, he's since gone legit, drives a Lexus, and owns real estate.

As articulate as my father can be, seeing me lying here on a gurney has left him at a loss for words. The skin on both of my legs is blackened, the bruising indistinguishable from the rubber streaks of the Samoan's front bumper. My left leg is exposed on some pillows and my knee is swelling at a disturbing rate with fluid.

"I'm okay, Dad," I say. Slowly, I shift the upper part of me on the gurney, being careful not to move my legs. I point to the x-ray of fuzzy bone matter clipped up on the lit board. "See? Nothing's broken. The doctor's already checked it out. He just thinks I seriously sprained it."

The x-ray and the ER doctor's reading do nothing to calm him. Instead they kick start him into panic mode. "*Ante pida ti mana sous,*" he mutters, looking all around, for what I'm not sure. My father isn't making sense. Somebody, apparently the ER doctor, needs to go do something perverted to his mother.

Too fired up, too hurt and angry, I see the helplessness of my condition, the helplessness of his, rushing up in his face. The last thing I want is for his eye to explode again, blinding him entirely.

"Dad," I say. "I'll be fine."

"Like hell you're fine." He rips the x-ray from the clipboard. The film makes a rippling sound like it could snap in two. "Look at you. Your knee looks like a goddamn melon. Where are your crutches?"

* * *

Truth is, we can't afford a second opinion, but I get one anyway, from a surgeon no less. Dr. Amaya is top notch and has operated on the L.A. Kings hockey team, the Clippers basketball team, and UCLA and USC football players too. Uncle Dimitri asked around and found him. The surgeon is doing a favor by taking me on as a patient when I have no insurance, a favor he will most likely want to take back once my father's checks begin to bounce.

The MRI reveals that I'll need two pins in my knee and nearly an inch worth of bone filler to harden up in the shattered part of my shin. If all goes according to plan, my leg will once again be as long as the other and I should be able to walk without a cane or a limp. Of course this news does nothing to quell my anxiety that I'll be the only junior at Cal State Bernardino seen dragging her leg around campus as if, like the hunchback character Quasimodo I've studied in a lit class, I'm on my way to the clock tower.

"You'll be just fine," Dr. Amaya says. "At least you're in for some big money. By the looks of that water balloon on your knee, she must've been drag racing."

I nod, not about to let it be known that the Samoan can't be found. Turns out her license was expired, her plates too, and when the cops asked for her home number she gave them a 1-800 one which she claimed was her work.

That night, after we return from the doctor's, against my father's better judgment, he tries the number and holds out the phone so I may hear. The voice on the other end is a taped recording for free information on log cabin homes built for under fifteen grand in the Louisiana bayous.

* * *

The surgery takes place down on the basement floor of Dr. Amaya's clinic. With such high profile patients, it only makes sense he has his own operating room. Even though his office is in Beverly Hills the fact I'm not in a hospital makes it seem like I'm south of the border, in Tijuana or Brazil, getting a cheap nose job or breast implants.

Afterward, when I come to, I'm face to face with the man who put me out, the anesthesiologist, actually more than one of him. I'm seeing blurry doubles—two manicured beards, two sets of shallow green eyes. I feel him take hold of my wrist. I feel him thumb my pulse.

"How are you feeling, Paula?"

My injured leg is mummified in gauze and the other is in some kind of brown cross between nylons and a knee-high sock that's cutting off all circulation. Beforehand it was explained that I'd either wake up crying or cranky, and even in my drug-induced state I instantly know which mood I'm in by the way I grab the v-neck of the man's scrubs, along with some of his salt and pepper chest hair.

When he winces, I only pull harder.

"Get this off me," I demand. My post-op tantrum knows no bounds and with all my might I hoist my good leg a near inch or two off the gurney. "Do I look like the kind of girl who wears flesh colored pantyhose?"

My father, not the nurse, pushes me by wheelchair out of the clinic and to the car. On the drive back to Rex's house, my father stops off at his lawyer's office in Pasadena, the woman who represents him with the State Bar. He cracks the car windows as if like a dog or a baby I might suffocate. I'm still reeling from the anesthesia that has yet to wear off, and he could be in there for five minutes or five hours. But when he returns to the car I clearly see his face is all wrong at the news the State Bar is ready to settle.

"Those *poutanas* expect me to sell Secret Wish and admit to something I never goddamn did."

The horse he paid forty grand for is now worth half a million and change. All it took was a lap around the Celebration stadium with a horseshoe of flowers adorning the animal's neck. Standing in the winner's circle, along with Secret Wish and Rhea's secret lover Dumbo, was our last photo taken as a family.

I shut my eyes, hoping my father will think I'm sleeping. He isn't big on conceding he's ever made a mistake, which is why he stands little chance in ever getting my mother back. When she heard I'd been hit by a car, she burst into tears, rushing into the reasons why she couldn't possibly fly out. Nicholas. Rhea. Her new job answering customer complaints at Duck River Electric. Saying I understood was the only way to stop her from listing everything in her life that's above me. Of course there might be more to it. There might be the consequences she would most likely face seeing my father again after having recently found out she's moved on with another man, a farmer no less, who, with his denim suspenders, rubber boots, and mini-tractor, fits seamlessly into my mother's new rural lifestyle.

My father starts the car and gains his distance, his resentment building with every mile at the State Bar forcing his hand. What any other lawyer in deep trouble would see as a way out, my father sees as defeat.

* * *

For the next week and a half I lay trapped in my parents' old bed with a torturous machine I've nicknamed The Mussolini, after the rabid Italian dictator. The muscles in my leg have already shut down and in order for my knee to regain all flexibility, every morning I must strap it in The Mussolini and adjust the knob that controls the range of motion in which it will be mechanically bent—increasing it by five degrees each day.

My father can't bear to watch and before he goes to work he leaves two prescribed Vicodin and a glass of water spiked with a shot of ouzo to wash them down with. I only take one pill, sometimes I take none and simply sweat out the pain because I don't want to become addicted.

Sometimes I leave my leg in there for an extra hour simply because I want to speed things up and be back to normal and back in school as soon as possible. The times when I am forced to get out of bed are even more excruciating. Crutches propping me upright, a fifteen foot trip to the bathroom takes over half an hour one way. Rex doesn't work and agreed to be home during the morning shift when my father's at the office. He agreed to lend a hand and help me out of bed or pass me my crutches, basically making sure that if I tip over I don't spend the rest of the day twitching like road kill in the hallway. Only Rex is never here.

Shortly after my father leaves, Rex goes too, fringed in leather from the chaps, to the vest, to the tie around the wisp of his balding man's pony tail. He jabs his head in the doorway, never stepping in the sick room, which smells like a giant Band Aid. Over the years he's grown a goatee as if hair on his face offsets what he lacks on his head.

"I'm meeting my new lady friend at IHOP," he says. "All you can eat pancakes." His joke is a distasteful reference to his passion for morbidly obese women. "I'll be home in a couple hours."

What he means is he won't return until right before my father gets back. He's uncomfortable with me being here, and while I want nothing more than to leave, I'm hardly in any condition to get to the restroom much less out the front door. Rex's mental state may not be so apparent on the exterior, but it most definitely shows in his choice of interior decor. Besides the Harley, his living room looks like the garden center at Target—a brand new rider lawn mower stands in for a couch and in one corner of the entryway, like a potted plant, is a top of the line weed whacker.

"You sure you don't want that crazy bitch tracked down?" Rex asks. He cocks his head to the side and bangs the doorframe a couple of times with his fist. "Me and some buddies could give her a little refresher course on a pedestrian's right of way."

The picture of the fiercest motorcycle gang in the world chasing down the Samoan, surrounding her blue hatchback with their low roaring hogs, is tempting. But I don't want to get my hopes up. The "buddies" Rex is referring to might be the imaginary voices he hears if he forgets to take his meds.

"I appreciate the offer," I say. "But my dad says I've got to let it go. I'm supposed to focus on my recovery."

Rex snorts on his way out, as if my father's advice that he once paid through the nose for is now something worth laughing at.

* * *

In the bathroom that night when the toilet is on the fritz, I'll find a packet of white powder taped conveniently inside the tank, in case the cops come calling. My father isn't back from work yet. He doesn't like coming home to a home that isn't his. I'm sure he doesn't know Rex is dealing dope, but I want him to. I want him to leave here, to find a place of his own even if it's a studio apartment with no room for me and I have to heal up at the old Portuguese lady's house.

From the outside patio there is cheering and clapping. Rex has company. He's holding a support group for overeaters, what he calls a "cattle call," where celery and carrot sticks and bottles of water are served. He shares his own bogus weight loss story, gaining the trust of the most vulnerable fat women who will give him their numbers after the meeting.

My father and I are the only ones who use this bathroom and before I hobble back to bed, I tear off and plug enough paper in the bowl that even a plunger couldn't clear.

Much later I'll be awakened to something like an argument or maybe the TV with the sound turned up too loudly. Maybe it's both because nobody wants me to listen. I think I hear my father's voice. I think I hear Rex's. Something about a loan or wanting to be alone. For a moment the two of them sound like a couple in the heat of a romantic break-up. My father must've found the drugs or they're fighting about something they both have a claim on. Only being screwed out of money or screwing another man's woman bring men to such rage. Since my father is not big on large women, this might be all business—apples and almonds.

In time I will learn that my father has accused Rex of skimming the profits, close to a hundred grand, and because my father is in such a spot, because no one will believe a lawyer who's under investigation by the State Bar, Rex will get away with it. I'll find the proof filed away in a metal cabinet when I'm clearing out my father's storage unit shortly after his death. The groves that were valued at a couple million, Rex will write my father a check for a few grand as a settlement, a decimal of what is owed him, and they will part with the kind of deep-rooted bitterness that only comes from enemies that were once friends.

Before I reach for my crutches, the house is quiet again.

The next morning, Rex and my father are gone like usual and there are no traces of a knock-down drag-out fight—no broken glass or dishes, no fist holes in the walls. The back yard equipment still stands upright in the living room, the weed whacker leans by its handle in the entryway, as do the recently purchased set of tiki torches, and I'm almost convinced by the sheer lack of physical evidence that I dreamed the whole thing. But I know different. I know my father, and he will be packed up and gone before I return later that day from an appointment with Dr. Amaya, an appointment he forgets all about. I drive myself with the seat reclined to stretch out my leg and enough pillows behind my back to stuff me in position at the wheel.

When I get home that evening his Mercedes diesel isn't parked in the driveway so I continue on and cruise past the local Motel 6 on Katella Avenue. His car isn't there. Next I go to the Bicycle Club all the way in Bell Gardens, a good half hour's drive, where my father sometimes waits out the night when he can't sleep, betting on cards. I don't find him there either. I also don't find him in front of Uncle Dimitri's two bedroom cottage in Belmont Shore, the cozy little beach town where Erick also lives. When I do find my father's car it will be in the last place I can think to look—parked in the driveway at Yia Yia's house right beside Psycho Gil's dark blue Mercury Cougar.

This comes as a complete shock, just as my mother had done to me years before when I was left with mere minutes to decide if I wanted to go with her to live in Tennessee or stay with my father. Where she gave me the illusion that I had a choice in the matter, my father has ditched me altogether. Though I will continue to try, part of me has never fully been able to forgive either one of them.

I see my father going home to his mother and the brother who lusted after his own sister-in-law and eventually took out that sexual obsession on her own two young daughters as the worst form of betrayal. The disappointment I feel for my father is crushing, it weakens my grip on the wheel, and I drive away more heartbroken than I have ever felt or will ever allow myself to feel again.

THE OPENING

My relationship with Professor Brown turns personal at the same time I start dodging my father's calls. I won't pick up, not just because I know where he's staying. As I feared Dr. Amaya has sent the rest of my fifteen thousand dollar bill to collections and men who call themselves Forrest Green and John Johnston are leaving rude messages. "Pay up, Loser," one of them says, "or else you'll never buy another car or get another credit card for the rest of your life. Even bankruptcy can't save you."

Threats over money are worthless if you're broke, if your part-time job at a lotion and bubble bath store barely covers the rent, if tuition and books are paid with student loans and breakfasts consist of Pop Tarts and dinners are flavored rice packets, two for a dollar. I'm getting around just fine now without crutches, without a limp. Hardly even a scar. On Saturday nights Lucia and I go out to Mimi's Cafe where I splurge on a turkey burger just for the meat.

My father assumes I already know where he's staying. Psycho Gil must've seen me with his night vision goggles. My father wants me to come over for dinner, Yia Yia misses me, like there's a statute of limitations in the Priamos family for sexual molestation and incest and everybody else is past it, everybody but me. If my father has his reasons for moving in with Yia Yia and Psycho Gil I'm not ready to hear them. He could've stayed with Uncle Dimitri, there's even a spare room at the Portuguese woman's home where I rent a room. He could've done a lot of things besides sell me and my sister out.

My brief chats with Professor Brown after class intensify in the halls and turn into shared confidence by the time we reach his office, before I sit down on the loveseat he uses to nap on in between classes, and he closes the door. His eyes are what draw me in—dark and vulnerable—like a hurt little boy, their smallness offset by the longest set of lashes any woman would envy. Without having read any of his writing I sensed at first glance that he'd seen too much in his life early on, a suspicion that will eventually be confirmed after I read all of his books. Unlike others who've mined their own personal tragedies time and time again in thinly veiled novels, it doesn't appear Professor Brown has come any closer to finding catharsis or peace. He seems forever haunted by his past. His near childlike anguish at his age in middle life intrigues me.

It keeps me coming back to his cramped office where we talk about my writing, we talk about his. He's having trouble getting another book off the ground, something to do with being too preoccupied with the stresses of his home life. He has a wife, some sons, and a rumored problem with the bottle. Since he's a rare species in the English department with his mountain man look of Levis and work boots, many of his students, most of them women, gossip why he never wears a ring.

Part of me wants him to strictly stay my mentor. He says he sees talent in me and has used and copied a couple of my stories as examples in class. I pay attention to his advice on writing, the three strikes rule—a writer must bring something up three times for it to stick in the reader's mind. The other part of me stares too hard at what I should be ignoring. I stare at his forearms that within a few short weeks have muscled up like a horse's hind leg.

"Steroids," I tell my hunch to my sister on the phone one night. She's pregnant and calls late when she has heartburn from the baby, from the father of her unborn child who works at Jack Daniels Distillery in Lynchburg and doesn't come home until well after the bars close. If it weren't for the time difference and her boyfriend being an alcoholic, she might not call so regularly. "His arms don't hang straight at his sides like other guys. The muscles of his upper body make them flare out. How else could his arms get that big so fast?" I ask her.

Her end is silent, and I hear a gurgle in her throat. She clears it.

"You're thinking about him too much," she finally says. "You should hear yourself. Isn't he married?"

"Wasn't Dumbo?"

Rhea takes a loud sip of something. The adolescent nickname I gave her first adult-sized crush still proves irritating. She drinks a lot of fluids just like our mother when she was pregnant with Nick. At nearly six months, Rhea's baby is already seven pounds. She'll probably have it cesarean. They're so close they even share the same pregnancy symptoms.

"The last thing you should be doing is comparing what I've already done with what you'd like to do. We're two different people. Besides," my sister adds like she's dead serious. "An affair isn't all that it's cracked up to be. Hands down, those were the longest fifteen seconds of my life."

* * *

Professor Brown signs two copies of his novels and a collection of short stories for me, and when I'm done reading those late at night or during my breaks at Bath & Body Works, he gives me some of his favorite writers' books. He gives me Ernest Hemingway's A *Moveable Feast*, a nonfiction account of his drinking days in Paris with other writers like Gertrude Stein and F. Scott Fitzgerald, a paperback I already own but am not about to let on that I do. He gives me an advance copy of Tim O'Brien's *In the Lake of the Woods*, a dark love story about a Vietnam War vet who may or may not be responsible for his wife's disappearance. And it's signed by the author—To Jim and Holly, Peace. Holly. I hadn't known her name before then. Inked permanently with her husband's in the inside cover is the first proof she's flesh and bone, since only school pictures of their three boys are tacked to the cork board above his desk, all of whom look like him. It's enough to almost make me return the book before I do any more damage to the spine.

In her husband's class I want to prove myself and go well beyond what's required, like when I drag Lucia with me and together we track down author Robert Stone, pinning him at the podium after a talk he gives at the *Los Angeles Times* Book Festival on the UCLA campus. Without the mic on, I get him to admit that his mother who'd been in and out of insane asylums was the inspiration behind the beautiful and disturbed actress in one of his novels, which I'm giving an oral report on. Shortly after filming a scene in Mexico, the actress theatrically walks out into the rough waters of the Pacific, drowning herself in front of her lover and costar. The quote impresses Professor Brown like I know it would.

It is not the typical affair, not in the physical sense. There is no sex, at least not right away, while I'm still his student. But it's emotional, which proves far more dangerous. He is outraged when he hears about how my mother only gave me forty-five minutes to leave with her for Tennessee. That she took my baby brother and he's grown up this long with only sporadic visits from his father. He's outraged that my father went home to his mother and pedophile brother and expects me to break out the feta cheese and ring bread with them as if nothing happened.

"Your father doesn't deserve such a smart, talented daughter like you. Brother or no brother, he should've beat the hell out of that sick fucker." Already Professor Brown sounds entirely too protective of me, and I like this about him, his tough talk, the masculinity in his voice, the inappropriateness of him passing such unrelenting judgment on my father after only hearing my side. He's nothing like the younger guys I've dated who cowered in my father's presence or dashed like a mouse off the front porch when he turned on the lights. Professor Brown is no boy. He could go toe to toe with a mugger off the streets and odds are I'd get to keep my purse.

"I'd tell you about my family," he says. "But most of them are already dead. My brother took his own life. My father died of cancer. Oh, yeah," he adds like a joke, minus the punch line, "my mother went to prison when I was five for setting fire to her family's apartment building and an old woman died." Arson and murder are no laughing matters, and he knows it. His story is sobering, which explains why he's a drinker. The past is too painful to reconcile clear-eyed, and therefore the most upsetting parts are relived over and over again, muted and then magnified by the consumption of the bottle the way I watched my father torture himself at the kitchen table with the family slides, the projector and his tumbler of ouzo.

"Your life story kind of sounds like the lyrics to a country song," I say, teasing him, flirting badly, the only way I know how. We're alone in the classroom after I've given my report. The fluorescents are turned off because bright lights hurt his eyes. The quarter is officially now over and Professor Brown lets me see the A in red ink next to my name in his grade book.

Out of nowhere I kiss his prickly cheek. He just stands there as stunned as if I'd just slapped him. This is my first and only move on him, one I instantly retreat from. Never have I been so forward with any guy, and I'm embarrassed. I'm an idiot and with books in hand, I reach as casually as I can for the door with the other, a student just a little too grateful for her high grade.

In the hall he catches up with me and invites me back to his office. He shuts the door, he boots up his computer, focusing on the lit screen. One hand trembles. It's a little after four, his drinking hour, and he steadies it on the mouse.

"I'm not happy in my marriage, Paula," he says. "Neither one of us are. We haven't been for some time."

I don't need my father or Uncle Dimitri to tell me these words are the battle cry for practically every married man who's about to stray from his wife and family. They are the words that are supposed to give me hope. They are my opening. Professor Brown scrolls down on the screen and if I didn't know any better I'd think he was ignoring me so I'd leave.

"There's a writer's conference coming up at the end of the month in Reno," he says. "You could come as my guest."

* * *

Professor Brown and I are scheduled to take separate planes, separate airlines, which is all my idea. Already I'm thinking ahead to the painful return flight home, the intimate moments I'll relive in the solitary confinement of my window seat—the empty room I'll be coming back to, his house in the San Bernardino Mountains, full of family—a wife, three sons.

I'm at my gate and there's less than five minutes until boarding when the Southwest employee announces that the flight will be delayed at least an hour, maybe longer. The affair I'm having reservations about might not even happen. I'll miss my connecting flight from San Jose to Reno. I'll miss my first of only two nights with him because of thunderstorms in Amarillo.

The plastic boarding pass in my hand reminds me of a Do Not Disturb sign. I'm traveling light, just a duffel bag, a purse, and Morrison's *Beloved*. In my wallet is enough cash to get me on another plane, his plane. I set down my plastic pass. He'll probably pay for my meals anyway.

As I rush through the airport toward the American Airlines ticket counter, my chest is heavy with guilt, with anticipation. I'm already cheating in every part of my body that matters, my mind, my heart. The rest of me just needs to catch up and it will tonight in the hotel room.

After I pay for my ticket and request the seat next to his, I hide out at another gate until it's time to board. From where I'm standing, I watch him come out of the restroom in an ill fitting sports coat I've never seen him wear before with elbow patches. His face is pasty like he isn't feeling well and wet from splashing it at the sink. He turns a couple of times like somebody might be following him. But nobody is, only me with my eyes.

He has an aisle seat and his eyes change, surprised, in a good way when I push duffel first toward him.

"I thought you were on a different flight," he says, already out of his seat, and stowing my bag in the compartment above.

"I changed my mind," I say. "But my return flight is the same."

His sports coat is off and as I take the center seat, my hand drifts across the density of his back. Besides the cursory kiss on the cheek that afternoon in the classroom, this is the first time I've felt him, felt the muscle and mass of him. He is not lanky and light with his fingers like my guitarist ex-boyfriend Erick. He is a man with a bulky sports coat, a wife, kids, and a mortgage, and it's hard not to panic when the captain turns on the red seat belt sign, a warning of sorts that there's no getting out now. The flight attendants pull up on the doors before pulling down on their seats, preparing for takeoff.

During the flight we make up for lost time. He touches and touches my forearm, discovering his fingers between mine, then letting go, running his fingers up and down the length of my arm, tapping a beat in my palm. I can't keep up. His movements are so rapid that I don't know how to react. Instead I just stay still.

The flight attendant smiles politely. She wants to hand Professor Brown his second beer with a tiny bottle of vodka. If it's not the considerable gap in our ages it must be the lack of space between us that gives us away. She's probably seen our kind of couple one too many times. The weekend getaway. The affair to remember.

Later in our room at the hotel and casino he will throw a shirt over the lampshade, dimming the light. He will be paranoid and not only chains the door but looks around the room for something heavy. He finds it in the dresser and instead of pushing the piece of furniture across the room with both hands the way most people might, he turns it upside down, balancing it casually above his head like a native with a canoe.

"What are you doing?" I say.

"Ensuring our safety."

The Bible inside one of the empty drawers slides around as I watch the weightlifter in him heave once loudly before slowly setting the dresser down as if it were a bench press, right in front of the door. The floor thunders, then reverberates, and there is no telling what the people in the room below us must think is about to fall through the ceiling. Having my former professor essentially barricade us inside our hotel room is not how I imagined our first night together to go. I'm claustrophobic, not to mention a little freaked out.

"Nobody's going to barge in on us. The chain's on and I already hung the Do Not Disturb sign."

"Housekeeping isn't who I'm worried about," he says. "This is Reno. We're in a Holiday Inn. Any low life thief or drug addict could try and get in here."

Any drug addict is already in here. He claims it's only recreational use. He was nervous about going away with me and was under the assumption being unpredictably high would somehow make for better company. The drug is making him do strange things. He's not so much locking out others as he's locking us in. If, for whatever reason, I were to have to try and get away from him I couldn't. As if the heaviest piece of furniture in the room isn't enough protection, he stacks his suitcase, my duffel, plus my purse the size of a doctor's bag on top.

In bed when he reaches out for me, he instantly loses more than the desire to be sexually intimate. He loses all motor skills, including the use of his hands, which start to tremble uncontrollably like the rest of him as if he's gone into shock or a seizure. I thought he was just an alcoholic. Whatever this other substance may be, cocaine or meth, the high is winding down into flu-like symptoms—cold sweats and fever. I treat him like the sick man he is and wrap him in a blanket. Then I run a washcloth under the tap in the bathroom and cover his forehead with the cool compress.

"Sorry," he says. He is embarrassed at the tremors he can't stop, half of his face under the cuff of the covers. "I should've warned you what you were getting into. My wallet's in the back pocket of my Levis. If you want to get your own room."

His arms are impossible to lock mine around, so I square them at the tips of his shoulders. I hold him as if by my sheer will I will drive out all the toxins he's ingested, his demons too.

"No." There is no way I'm abandoning him to suffer alone through the ugliness of the drug wearing off. This moment is not so different from the day I found my father lying face down, lovesick and destroyed, on the floor of his office after my mother left. I don't care how naive or co-dependent or selfishly noble I sound. I don't leave men who need me. "I want to be here with you," I say.

This forty-year-old man, my professor, who I still can't seem to call by his first name, curls up into me. He shivers, the drug sweating out from his pores. His skin smells of plastic, of the various detergents and under the counter kitchen cleansers that are mixed together and heated up to be smoked. Weathering his withdrawal might bring us closer in a way that the best sex never could.

"I love you." He says this clearly as if there is no mistake, then his eyelids flutter as if he's exhausted enough for sleep.

The proof that I love him is right here in the way I hold him, in the way I haven't run. But I have to protect myself.

Saying he loves me has come out at the wrong time like gratitude, a thank you, and I pull away some. I close my eyes, closing myself off from what I didn't want to hear.

*   *   *

The next morning he's feeling better, less frantic, which only makes me more tense. Saying he loved me might've been an accident, an unspoken symptom of withdrawal, words meant for his wife, not me. Color, only too much of it now, comes back into his face. After breakfast we sit out by the pool—me in a tank and shorts, him dressed for higher altitudes in his mountain wear of work boots, Levis and a long-sleeved t-shirt. He's finishing off an essay that he's going to read in less than a half hour. It's about getting clean in South Dakota when he was a writer-in-residence a couple years back. Eventually this experience will become the final chapter in *The Los Angeles Diaries*, a memoir he'll publish years later.

Jim straddles the chaise lounge. In all those clothes, in his condition, the rising desert heat is getting to him. He wipes at his forehead with his sleeve. A pad of paper and a pencil are between his legs. For nearly an hour he's been writing and rewriting the same first lines of his essay, getting nowhere. The drug has left him too focused to see things clearly. I don't see how he'll make it in time for the reading.

"Maybe you should read something from *Luckytown*." The story is about a con man and his teenage son who steal a car and take it across the desert to cheat the tables in Vegas, the law in hot pursuit.

Jim shakes his head. Tiny wet hairs stick to the back of his neck.

He keeps his hair cut short which makes me think he's afraid he's losing some.

"Holly hates that book. She calls it the great American white trash novel."

"Holly isn't here."

The way I say her name sounds as insulting as her comment.

His wife is with us now and when Jim glances up from the pages, he can't hold my stare and looks away toward some kids splashing in the pool.

"Sorry. I shouldn't have said that."

"*She* shouldn't have said that."

"She was just angry," he trails off, running short on reasons to defend her, running even shorter on time. "I just need your help," he frets. "The rest will come out fine if I can just nail this line about my detoxing."

I roll over on to my stomach. I can't believe he doesn't see it.

"Like what you're doing *now?*"

Jim nods, scratching at his arms.

"It feels like ants. Ants keep crawling and crawling right beneath the surface of my skin. They won't goddamn stop."

"That's your line," I say. "About the ants."

"Nobody wants to read about insects, Paula."

"Why not?" I shade my eyes with my hand so I may better see him. With the other I press down on his knee reflexively bouncing at the heel like a wind-up toy. "You always say to write it like it is."

He smiles, the writer and professor part flattered at being quoted back to him. I want to ask how many female co-eds have taken this trip with him before me, but if men lie to their wives about having an affair, the last thing they'll do is tell the truth to their lovers. Jealousy burns in me like the fever I helped him break last night, and I take my hand off his knee.

The writer's conference is at this hotel, and in front of everybody poolside he leans across the space between us, he reaches out for me.

"Hey," he says, "you okay?"

"I'm fine."

"You don't look fine."

"Well, I am."

"You do realize I meant what I said last night. I love you."

"I love you too." I say this before I can think of all it's opened me up to, before my father and Uncle Dimitri have a chance to creep back into my head the way I realize they did last night.

Jim slides his hand gently behind my neck, pulling me in for an unapologetic kiss he will be sorry for later. There are too many others around us, other writers, agents, editors who are fully aware of his life back in Southern California. Obviously the drug has yet to wear off. Professor Brown is still delusional.

* * *

Our affair doesn't let up once we return. We only grow closer. We sneak in "I love you's" in the front seat of his red BMW as he circles the parking lot, pretending to look for my car. Or with the office door closed, curled up on his love seat, we talk, really talk, about the complicated possibilities of a future together. Sometimes I simply lighten up the mood by lapsing into raunchy jokes my father and Uncle Dimitri have told over the years and Jim laughs, surprised I know such men's locker room humor. We laugh together until the phone rings or I have to leave to work my shift at Bath & Body Works. As for any physical affection, it's strictly over the clothes. With a nosy female professor next door and heavy foot traffic outside in the hall, our couch time has certain restrictions. We even sneak in a quick lunch of hamburgers and chocolate shakes at Red Robin with my little brother who comes out for a visit, unafraid of how it looks to Nicholas that Professor Brown is taking us out for a meal.

Though this is my first and only affair with a married man, it's hard not to notice, it's hard not to feel that he's flirting with something more lasting with me. Weeks later when my landlady invites her problem son and his pregnant girlfriend to move in, Jim helps me find an affordable little one room cabin in Crestline, the same mountain town where he lives. Out in the front yard while he's helping me move, he puts his arm around my shoulders, a risky gesture considering it's a small community and his wife knows just about every woman in it but me. He even unloads an old mattress used by one of his kids and pushes my single in with the other, making a queen—big enough for the both of us should he ever decide to leave his wife.

WEIGHT AND MATTER

The night before I'm to leave for Tennessee to meet my sister's new baby girl, Annabelle, I find myself sitting beside Uncle Dimitri's latest girlfriend, a big breasted Cuban bombshell who breaks open a dinner roll and announces to the table that it smells like dirty feet. Vintage wines and lobster tail are served on table linens here in this restaurant, and I glance at the other diners to see if they overheard. We're at a window table in the clubhouse at Los Alamitos racetrack near Long Beach. Of all the major tracks in Southern California it's the most convenient, with a lesser amount of foot traffic than Santa Anita, Del Mar, or Hollywood Park. The VIP section overlooking the prime position of the finish line is Uncle Dimitri's second office, his second home. Although he is the one who called, it is my father who wants to see me. He doesn't like knowing I'll be spending time with my mother when the two of us are on the outs.

"Lo, Lo, Lo," Uncle Dimitri says. Her nickname alone elevates her one step above the average fling. He smiles with a toothpick in his mouth. "My niece would like to eat the rest of her shrimp cocktail here."

But I'm no longer hungry. I never was. I've lost nine pounds since I began the affair with Jim.

Another race is starting and the jockeys in their brightly colored silks look as if they're sitting like children on the saddles with their legs behind them as they rein their rides into the gates. Uncle Dimitri hardly notices, which means he hasn't bet on this race.

"So where is he?" I say. "You said seven, right?"

I suspect where my father must be but I want to hear it confirmed by somebody else. I've suspected for some time he may have a visual stimulus with no table etiquette like Lola. He may have several for all I know, the kind if he ever tried to touch he'd get beaten and thrown out on the street, the kind that look cool when working the stage under hot lights in spiked heels and g-strings. The signs are all there. While we still lived together at the Chino house, I picked up the ashy odor of cigarettes on his clothes—only he doesn't smoke. Possibly he was at the Bicycle Club, except that during a past due electrical bill blackout, I had rifled around in the dark searching for matches and lit a candle from a little black book I'd never seen before from a club called the Kat Nip. On the cover was a hot pink drawing of a busty half-naked, half-feline woman with tiny whiskers, a tail, and in tall stilettos.

"Your father's been pretty depressed lately," Uncle Dimitri begins. "Moving back in with my mom and Gil. Losing the house. Don't tear into him over it, Paula. He couldn't take that coming from you. He had nowhere else to go."

Apparently Uncle Dimitri never offered my father a room at his place, most likely because he wants privacy with Lola. Given his own brother took him in after having undergone a quadruple bypass, his lack of generosity when my father needs him most seems selfish. I like him a little less now.

"So where is he?" I ask again. "Or should I ask, who is she?"

"I only know her stage name," Uncle Dimitri says. "She's a bur-lesque dancer."

"Wonderful," I say, stopping myself from completing that thought at this table. Lola is a cocktail waitress, though I'm not sure where. The line between baring all and baring cleavage might be a thin one, and I don't want to offend. Well after their relationship has run its course and Lola leaves Uncle Dimitri for a younger man, I'll drop by his house and meet her illegal replacement. She'll be another young server but this girl hails from Mexico City and can't speak English. A man who's never been able to live alone, Uncle Dimitri will have boldly smuggled her across the border in the front seat of his BMW. She'll smile at me and disappear fast into a bedroom, knowing her place. When I watch her go it won't be her whom I'm thinking about. Fully recovered from surgery, Uncle Dimitri will always have a bad heart.

My father shows up at the table, loosening his tie as if it being too tight is what's caused his cheeks to flame, not the flask of ouzo that must be filling up the inside pocket of his jacket. He won't look at me. The patch is gone. He's seeing clearly now, though I'm not so sure he is about some things. Going to strip clubs is one thing, paying for more than a lap dance is quite another. He could be seeing more girls than the one Uncle Dimitri mentioned.

I know I'm being unfair, judgmental. Some of these women are just trying to get by—she might have a kid with no father, a sick mother at home, maybe she's even putting herself through school. So many others I imagine must have drug problems, pimp problems. My father is asking for the kind of trouble he's getting too old to fight his way out of.

"Some *vromopousta* stalled out in the fast lane on the 110," he says. His shoulders make the table a tight fit, and he bumps me as he sits down. He eyes my appetizer. "Better finish off that fresh shrimp, Paula Girl. Where you're going it'll be deep fried and served with ketchup."

During dinner there is safe small talk about Rhea's caesarean section and some good natured bad jokes about her baby girl sharing the same weight and measurements, my father points out, as Wilt Chamberlain as a baby.

"The Lakers will have their first female forward," Uncle Dimitri says as he pulls out an impressive wad of C-notes and hands me four. "Why don't you and Lola place some bets. Take some chances. There's never any money in odds on favorites. Only cowards bank on safe bets."

Lola and I head to the betting booths and when we return I'm close enough to overhear just why we were sent off together to begin with. Uncle Dimitri is doing all the talking. He's older than my father by two years and this gives him the right.

"You're running out of time, Paul. It's a slap on the wrist. Take the fucking deal."

* * *

My mother picks me up in her boyfriend's Ford 250 truck equipped with a rack in the rear window but no rifle.

His name is Ely and she found him one afternoon passed out, having driven his mini Bobcat tractor straight into the ditch in front of the house. It's a whole new kind of love. She says God sent him to her. Not the twelve pack of Bud that made him lose sight between the flat stretch of Highway 64 and a great big hole. My mother is flushed, her hair redder with age, and she's put on a few pounds. She's content, in the pink with love.

Her familiar hug, warm and comforting, doesn't last long enough. She pulls back to assess.

"You look like you lost weight," she says, getting the advantage on me before we even reach baggage claim.

"Are you happy?"

"I'm in school, Mom. I work. There isn't much time to feel anything but stressed."

My mother has always been able to question me in a way my father, even as a lawyer, can't.

"Something's going on. I've heard your message on your machine. You're leaving your whereabouts for someone to know your every move."

She stops short of outright accusing me of hooking up with a stalker. It isn't like her. Maybe my affair is one secret my sister actually kept from her. My mother doesn't drive us to the big white house on Highway 64. Instead she takes us to a dark brown one story on a dirt road, a sagging wire fence instead of a sturdy one made of wood. From the pasture I spot Nicholas on a four wheeler, doing donuts, churning up the earth, a couple of friends riding with him on back. None of them are wearing helmets. They're barefoot and in swimming trunks. My mother sees them and waves, saying nothing.

"What are we doing here?" I ask. "I'm not staying at your boyfriend's house." It would be the ultimate betrayal of my father, even though he's done the same to me by living with Yia Yia and Psycho Gil.

"I moved here last year."

"Last year?" All of those phone conversations and Rhea never said a thing. This house with its weak fence and paint that's splitting away at the window frames is no colonial estate on a thirty acre spread. It's not the Chino house either that my father let go into foreclosure so she wouldn't have to resort to moving for extra cash.

"I was afraid you'd tell your father," my mother explains. "You know you would have. Don't deny it either. He'd never have let me sell it."

My mother may know how to read me but I can see right through her. She's too determined to get away from me and up those creaky steps that may give for good under her weight or mine, that my father if he were still in the picture would've deemed too dangerous and paid someone to have fixed.

"What'd you need the cash for, Mom? The farm is worth ten times this place and you owned it free and clear."

My mother's grip is firm on that old railing like she's upset enough to uproot it, post to post. She has a farm woman's hands now, toughened and sun damaged. Just last week Rhea told me how our mother shot at real life vultures that had collected on the rooftop. A mare had gone into premature labor out in the pasture and they had come for the bloody afterbirth of a stillborn baby foal.

"He showed up there, Paula. Right on my doorstep at ten o'clock at night."

"Who showed up?"

"Richard, Beth Anne's ex-husband. He said he traveled two thousand miles just to see the place. Why would he come all the way out here unless he was threatening me? Believe me, I got the message. Don't you understand, I had to pay him off? Who knew when he might show up again."

She yanks open the screen door, then looks down at me at the foot of those broken down steps. "I didn't want him out to get me the way he's out to destroy your father. I have Nicholas to think of."

The screen door slaps closed before I have the chance to edge in behind her, let alone admit that I think she has been a good mother to my little brother. She's proven it by forsaking the big white dream house to pay off Beth Anne's rabid ex-husband. Giving him the money back was the right thing to do. It's what my father should've done if his obsessions for prestige and dominance in the Walking Horse industry hadn't blinded all rational judgment. By selling off his show fleet he might've salvaged his marriage, certainly his law license.

Inside the house Rhea sits at the kitchen table breastfeeding Annabelle. She is in a robe, slightly parted, the baby's head in between. My sister's face and hair are done, as usual. But she is changed. Giving birth has breathed new life into her, the kind of vibrancy that prescription pills and hour-long therapy sessions can't even come close to providing. Maybe coincidence or a touching gesture, the baby is wrapped up in the soft cotton Winnie the Pooh pajamas and blanket I sent. All I see is the most fragile part of her head, the part that's still tender, and I crouch down beside her, afraid she might get offered up for me to hold. I finger the sparse strawberry blond hairs. It's been years if ever that I've been this close to my sister.

"She's perfect," I say.

Rhea smiles at her baby, not me. My compliment is lost in the obvious.

"I thought we'd stay the night at the house, so you can spend more time with her."

Where my mother used to cook with oregano, she now douses everything with salt before frying it in lard. At dinner she warms up corn bread in a skillet. Instead of a side salad, she scoops up soupy beans and a slice of ham cured country style, loaded with so much salt it will never spoil, no matter how long the meat is left out.

Ely reclines in a La-Z-Boy in the family room watching football. He reminds me of Saint Nick, only skinnier. His hair and beard are white, his nose is bulbous from booze and red from working out in the sun. I'm cordial to him because my brother isn't.

When Nicholas comes inside the house, he gives me a big hug. His feet are grass stained and his skin smells of iron from his own sweat. "How ya'll doin'?" His syllables slide and pitch into one another, the Middle Tennessee drawl I can hardly understand. How he speaks sounds strange coming from a Greek. Some of his pale friends tease him about his Mediterranean skin color and call him "The Mexican."

"I missed you, big sis," he says to me as if in that split second, he doesn't anymore. In some ways he resents me then and always will for living so close to the father he only sees in summer. We look and act very much alike and I know not to push myself on him.

He takes his plate and eats in his room, tapping a racket with his fork along the way so that Ely can't hear the commentators remarking on the last play. If our family had been broken before my mother left, we at least came together at dinner. My mother serves Ely first, leaving his dinner and uncapping a fresh beer on a TV tray. The rest of us eat at the dining room table.

Before bed, while my sister is in the shower, and my mother is in the bedroom with Ely, I hear Annabelle crying in her carrier, the chest rattling kind. Desperately, she wants to be picked up. She wants help.

I lift her in my arms, I pat her diaper, I bounce her.

Nothing works. She squints at me with someone else's eyes, her father's I've yet to meet. I take her to the couch.

"It's okay, Annabelle," I whisper. "Mommy will be back soon."

The fact I've stopped moving momentarily keeps her from crying. Lying back, I unbutton the top two of my blouse and hold Annabelle against my chest. Her eyes close. They open, then close again. She's falling asleep to the rhythm of my breathing, the way I did so many years before when I came into her mother's bedroom that night with my sleeping bag after our parents took off to Yia Yia's house in the hay truck loaded down with all of Psycho Gil's office equipment and tanks of Liqui-Steal. My beautiful baby niece will never know the Priamos side of the family. And I will make certain they will only know her through pictures.

The phone rings a couple of times and someone in another room picks up. My mother soon enters, carrying the cordless. She seems taken aback maybe by who is on the other end or the baby all curled up on my chest. I've never desired to have kids, never played with dolls.

"It's for you," she says, suspiciously, with the slightest tone of satisfaction in being right. "He says his name's Jim."

I take the phone and turn my head toward the couch.

"How'd you get this number?" I ask, careful not to move the rest of my body, hoping the jump in my heartbeat doesn't wake up Annabelle. My mother has not gone far, only into the kitchen to give me the illusion of privacy.

"Please don't be angry," he starts, "but I'm in your place. I came in through a window." The line snaps with static, the near two thousand miles of cable that connects our voices.

"You broke in?"

The baby lifts her head, then drops it again, the slightest human pressure of weight and matter on my chest.

I can hardly breathe. There's a blast of breath in my ear. Jim sounds closer than ever.

"I miss you."

"I miss you too."

"No," he says. "You don't understand. I'll be here when you come back. I don't want to be away from you anymore. I've left her."

WHAT THEY TOLD ME AFTER HE DIED

You have to stop thinking about what happened. You need to think about me. You need to think about *us*. Maybe you should talk with someone.

—Jim Brown

I don't give out information about my girls, but I can tell you I've never had a dancer here who goes by that name. I don't know who you've been talking to. Hope you haven't been offering up any cash with those questions of yours.

—Nigel Watkins, owner of the Kat Nip

Shut up. *Just shut up.*

—Psycho Gil

He died of natural causes. That's what it says on his death certificate.

—Yia Yia

Grief can act as a confessional, truth serum, if you will. It sounds like you got some necessary things off your chest. You know, we're not always supposed to maintain relationships that aren't healthy for us.

—Warren Lynstrom, Psychologist

Your father kept hoping there'd be a way out, another legal loophole he could slip through. There were so many times when he could've copped a deal and didn't. That afternoon when he came back from the hearing it was in his eyes, relief or despair, I'm not sure which. I had already cleared out my desk.

—Nora

CONDUCT UNBECOMING

The first time I see my boyfriend's estranged wife is in the rearview mirror while I'm driving down the deadliest strip of Highway 18 called The Narrows. There are no turn outs, no emergency lanes. Rocks and pine trees rise up on one side of the road, while the opposite side is a cliff that drops off thousands of feet. Getting so close to my bumper is no accident. Clearly she wants to put a scare into me. She wants to send me over the edge.

I know it's her by the hood of her SUV. For the past several months I've seen that hood, fading white like a water stain, of the black Toyota Forerunner pull into our drive every weekend when she leaves and picks up the kids. Jim and I have moved into an already furnished two bedroom rental, somebody's weekend getaway. I see the car and I hear her saying things like "So this is your love nest where you coop up with your little slut." Yet I never see her. Before she ever gets out, I always move away from the window, from the semblance of family as Jim goes outside and greets her and kisses each of their three boys on the head.

It's early, not even six thirty. She works part-time at Two-Toned, the local gym in Twin Peaks where Jim still works out. There's no reason for her to be behind me except actions speak louder than the harassing phone calls that are just talk. Whore. Cunt. Home Wrecker. The names I've grown used to hearing. Never have I fought back, because in her mind and partly in mine, I am all these things. I deserve it. I am the other woman. No matter how bad their marriage may have been it had been good once and I took the chance away from her ever getting that back again.

Steadily in the rearview mirror Holly's face takes shape. She's wearing sunglasses and her mouth moves like she's shouting to herself. Nobody is in the passenger seat. She's bumping it up to another level with the front bumper of her SUV, and I brace my hands at the wheel for the push that jerks the right side of my car toward the side of the mountain. My side mirror is nicked clean off. "You crazy psycho bitch," I cry out. I flip up my rearview mirror so she doesn't get any satisfaction in watching me flip out.

After one more hairpin turn the lanes divide into two on either side. Changing into another lane does nothing to stop the grill of her SUV from growing inside my rear window. She's expecting my every move.

We drive like this for the rest of the way down, miles upon miles of curving road, the straight-aways where she guns the gas and catches up, the sharp turns where I lose her again. Alongside the road are a flurry of wooden crosses, makeshift memorials with dying flowers and shrunken balloons. Just last week the fog moved up over the ridge and a young couple lost all sense of direction and rolled their vehicle right off the side of the road, the guard rail giving in from the force like a tin can. The girl wasn't wearing her seatbelt and was thrown from the car into the brush while her boyfriend hurled inside thousands of feet down to a place that took a helicopter, two bloodhounds and their handlers until dawn to find. Somehow the girl with a dislocated shoulder and a concussion climbed her way back up the mountain and flagged down a passing vehicle. Her heroic efforts made the front page of the *Mountain News* and her boyfriend was memorialized on the marquee at the movie theater.

By the time we reach the stoplight at the base of the mountain, Holly pulls up alongside me and honks, two light taps like I'm a friend she's just come across. Although I know better than to look, I do it anyway and that's when I see him, Holly and Jim's three year old son, Kyle, strapped in the backseat—his eyes full of fear, his mouth full of cracker. The light flicks green, his head wobbles back and Holly makes an illegal hard left in front of a UPS truck. He swerves to avoid her, and a small package tumbles out. Holly's hauling it back up the mountain.

To try and calm down, I pull out my cell and call my sister. Rhea has recently moved back home after her boyfriend stumbled into the bathroom one night, aggressive and amorous and reeking of alcohol. He insisted that he join her in the tub. Just as she was climbing out, he fell in backward, grazing his head against the soap dish, groggily conscious. She saved him from possible drowning by draining the water, then fled in only a bathrobe with the baby to my mother's house.

"What'd you expect?" my mother breaks in because she can hold it in no longer. I should question why she's been on the line this entire time, but my sister is living in her house and therefore part of my mother's rules apparently include listening in on phone calls. "You took this woman's husband, Paula. Of course she's going to come after you. This is the price you pay for having stayed with your father." She lets out a hearty sigh. "I hope I don't sound too critical, honey, because I love you. But you're just like him. You cheat."

*   *   *

The high school where I teach sits atop a brittle hillside on the border between San Bernardino and Los Angeles County in Diamond Bar. Considered a modern architectural landmark, the buildings are constructed of cool concrete, the corners cut sharp with mere slivers of darkened glass for students to be less distracted since they can hardly see out. The district supplements the sports teams by renting the school out as a location for films and car commercials.

Before pulling into the faculty parking lot, I hang up with my sister. Shortly after becoming a substitute I've taken over five freshman English classes mid semester because the teacher, a woman in her forties who was prone to growing facial hair, literally ran out of the classroom screaming after a couple of boys chanted "Sasquatch, Sasquatch!" There was more to it, of course. There were mid-quarter grades she failed to complete. With thirty-five students to a class and no means of discipline except for a pad of detention slips, she stopped trying to teach them anything and instead resorted to having them memorize and spell back to her list after list of vocabulary words.

On an emergency credential, I'm determined to prove to the administration I'm a safe bet. In class we've read aloud Shakespeare's *Romeo and Juliet*, both the Middle and Modern English versions out of the text, having the students play the characters, acting the roles in and out of their seats, soliloquies saved for standing on top of a chair. Whoever nails their lines best we vote on and that student gets to leave a couple minutes early from class. For a little downtime while I grade their essays, I put on the film version, the MTV version starring a young Leonardo DiCaprio with bangs and Claire Danes with darker hair and doe-eyed innocence. They play the desperate young lovers in a modern-day Verona, a gaudy and colorful suburb of Mexico City. Banana yellow souped-up convertibles. Sea blue low riders. Instead of hand to hand combat with knives and swords, there are shoot outs and fiery explosions at gas stations, guys with tattoos on their bald heads, transvestites dancing around in floppy curled wigs.

While I'm collecting their homework the phone rings. Reggie picks up. He's the star three point shooter on the basketball team who last week I caught leaning for answers during a test and now sits closest to my desk.

"Yo, Ms. P.," he says. He tilts his head to the side like the bill of his baseball cap. "Some lady with a funked out voice."

I assume it's my sister calling back, the Middle Tennessee dialect she picked up fast and slowed down her syllables. My mother likes to leave a few days between insults to forgive and forget.

"What's up Rhea?"

"Rhea? I'm not your Tennessee 'ho' of a sister."

It's Holly, faking a drawl that sounds more like a bad attempt at a Spanish accent. How she got this number, I don't know. The calls have always been to the house, never here. Jim must've mentioned to her where I work. The two of them must've talked about me. Figuring out I'm part of their small talk upsets me in a way that her tracking me down in my classroom or trying to run me off the road hasn't. It upsets me in a way that makes me mean.

"What do you want besides your husband back." I say this low so that Reggie and the rest of my students don't hear.

On screen Juliet is out on her bedroom balcony, distraught, having just found out she's fallen for the son of her family's most dangerous rival. She throws herself forward and for a moment it seems as if she might let more than just her anguish over him go. "My only love," she implores, "sprung from my only hate."

Holly laughs. "I want you to see Jim the way I do. He's a no good son of a bitch. He left his wife and three sons for Christ's sake. What makes you think he won't leave you?"

*　*　*

That afternoon I don't drive home because I am bound for Lakewood, a forgettable little tree-lined suburb of Los Angeles that touts as its claim to fame being the birthplace of the first Denny's restaurant. I've finally accepted Yia Yia's dinner invitation. Recently she had hip surgery. Now in place of brittle bone a steel plate and screws join with her pelvis. Twice in the hospital her fever spiked and she was kept for nearly six weeks, treated for infection. "People her age die from this," my father adds, putting his own screws to me. "She asks about you, you know. Why you won't come by and see her."

Breaking her hip isn't what gets me. It's the way that it happened. Yia Yia had been tending to her garden and fell getting up off her knees. Nobody was home, not my father or Psycho Gil. Although neither of them work, they were driving to the post office in the industrial city of Vernon where Psycho Gil keeps a box. He wants to deceive potential buyers into assuming there's a fully operational factory that manufactures Liqui-Steal. Under the hot sun Yia Yia crawled several feet across the grass to the side gate where she lay beside garbage cans, running out of voice, calling for help. Close to four hours passed before one of the next door neighbors, a twin set of twenty something stoners who still live at home, heard her faint cries.

As I drive through Yia Yia's one story housing tract I notice Psycho Gil and my father walking in the park, engrossed in conversation, strategizing no doubt between the jungle gym and the monkey bars the next move with Liqui-Steal. My father has been out of work since the last hearing when the judge recommended his law license be taken. Subsequently he fired his lawyer and has written his own appeal. Now he's waiting to hear back from the three member Review Board. It's a weekday and I find it hard seeing him dressed like Psycho Gil for the weekend.

Gone are my father's dry cleaned suits and the paisley ties I used to steam iron for him. My father and Psycho Gil in their shorts and sandals look like they're next up for a spirited game of shuffleboard. The only difference between them is a cell phone that's attached in a protective case on Psycho Gil's hip.

Yia Yia greets me at the door as if nothing has happened, the years we spent apart were never lived. Her scalp is visible, her thinning hair teased high as if she's fresh out of the salon chair and it hasn't had time to settle. We hug carefully because there is more between us than two generations of Greeks. There's the knowledge that she refuses to believe her son ever put his hands all over my sister and me. No matter how many other female relatives will eventually surface with similar stories, she will go to her grave calling us all either confused or outright liars.

"I hear you're dating an older man," she says as I step into the foyer. You can always tell if you're on Yia Yia's grudge list by whether your picture is hanging up on the family room wall. Mine is there, right next to my twin cousins' senior high school pictures, two of Uncle Dimitri's four sons. Rhea and Nicholas aren't—banished along with our cousin, Psycho Gil's daughter, in the hallway which rarely sees much light. The picture of me is a color 8 X 10 taken in Kindergarten. My hair is down to my waist and I'm wearing a white apron dress with Winnie-the-Pooh and Eeyore characters clustered down the sleeves. My smile is big with baby teeth. It occurs to me, it sickens me, that it might not have been Yia Yia who put up this picture. Psycho Gil may like them as little as five years old.

"His name's Jim Brown," I say to Yia Yia. "He's a professor."

She shrugs at something about him she already doesn't like.

"You might want to keep your last name if you marry. You're a Greek, not a pilgrim."

Spite and injury weigh heavily on the rest of her skeletal frame. She hunches over, moving across the pea green carpet and around her floral print furniture with a cane, not the walker her doctor prescribed. "My kitchen is too small to try and cook with a metal cart in my way," she explains, heading right for it. Even at seventy-nine Yia Yia is too practical to be handicapped. I make coffee and she sets out a Tupperware container of Greek pastries—baklava and my favorite Koulourakia shortbread cookies with sesame seeds sprinkled on top she's made from scratch.

While I dunk the cookies in coffee, she shows me snapshots of her trip to Greece Uncle Dimitri paid for. She shows me craggy headstones in tall grass where her father is buried up in the hillside, her mother too in the whitewashed sea port town of Nafplio in the Peloponese. In another picture Greek dancers are skipping sideways in an arc, tiny lit lanterns above them, the men in balloon pants and black vests. The women dressed like peasants, their faces bare and their heads under scarves. Some are smiling while others look like their mouths are shaped in the middle of an "opa!"—an exclamation of enjoyment used when dancing or shattering plates.

Before my father and Psycho Gil return from their power walk at the park, I'm out on the patio on purpose so I won't have to see them walk through the front door together. My father's head has always been too big for a baseball cap or anything else to fit properly and this afternoon he balances a visor on the crown. He reads through Jim's divorce papers, another reason why I agreed to come over. Jim trusts Holly and agreed to have her lawyer draw up the settlement, saving money by not getting his own.

With a pen my father marks up the margins the way I do grading student essays. "What the hell is this," he says every other second, writing "no, no, no" at Holly's lawyer requesting that Jim give her the house free and clear and he take the two small lots on the side.

"He wants her to have everything," I explain. "He feels bad for leaving."

My father shakes his head and scribbles some more.

"*Natophisas.*"

"You didn't write that, did you?"

My father smiles poker style. He's wearing a pair of sunglasses and all I see in the dark discs are miniature versions of myself.

"When the hell am I going to meet Professor Wonderful?" he says.

"Soon."

"You still afraid to answer your own goddamn phone?"

I tell him what I haven't yet told Jim.

"She followed me down the mountain this morning."

My father stops writing. I don't need to see his eyes to understand how disappointed he is in my weakness. I'm not acting like his daughter that would fight back at any cost. I'm acting like a woman that's deaf, dumb, and nearly blindsided literally by love.

"You're filing another police report on your way home tonight," he says. "Then you're getting a temporary restraining order like I've told you to goddamn do for months now."

With his urging I've already filed two reports—one for the relentless phone calls, up to twenty-five a night, and another for having coached her three-year-old to kick me in the leg as hard as he could while we were on the floor binding Legos together. When I asked him why he did it, he threw up his hands and circled me again and again, shouting, "Mommy say kick ho, Mommy say kick ho" like it was a twisted game she'd taught him.

"Jim says a restraining order will only make it worse."

My father laughs and shakes the divorce papers in his hand like he would his fist and I'm afraid what Greek curse word he's about to call the man I love next. "You're going to listen to someone who's dumb enough not to hire his own lawyer during a divorce? You're my daughter. If he won't protect you, then I will."

The sound of my father losing his temper draws Psycho Gil to the screen the way he was that afternoon watching me as I sat on the diving board, waiting to dry out from beneath his wet hands, the back of my shirt stuck to me like skin from the baby oil. I smell the pipe tobacco, the suntan lotion. Dinner is not an option—the confrontation put off again. In a minute I'll come up with an excuse and leave through the side gate.

"Fine," I say, aware of my audience. I pull out a stapled packet from my purse. "I'll do it if you agree to fill this out."

"What is it?"

"An application to take the CBEST so you can start subbing. You have to do something while waiting around for the Review Board."

"To hell with my license, Paula Girl. I'm better off without it. I know you don't like him but Liqui-Steal is really taking off. Last month Gil flew out to Palestine to spray it on some tanks."

"Palestine?" I say. To me, the substance touted as Liqui-Steal looks just like store-bought paint. "Are you sure he wasn't just down the freeway in Pacoima?"

My father talks over my sarcasm with his hands, all sweeping gestures like when he was going to clean up in Molokai, cornering all the tourist trade by building a hotel right smack in the middle of the island.

"I'm telling you," he insists, "I'm having one of my feelings."

I'm familiar with his feelings, the same feeling that buoyed him into buying a colonial estate, a forty thousand dollar horse, and some Hawaiian property in under seventy-two hours, the same feeling that has cost him his law license.

"Have they ordered any?" I ask. "The Palestinians?"

"Bureaucracy moves slow, Paula Girl."

"Right. What about that farmer? He flew Psycho Gil out to test spray his tractor. Where's his order? Lost in the mail for the past ten years or did the CIA intercept it?"

I'm scared of what's happening to my father. I'm scared of just how far he'll follow his brother into the alarming fantasy of FBI wiretaps, bullet proof vests, hand guns, Leer jets, and Middle Eastern wealth.

"Dad," I say. "I don't want you to lose it." Even as I say it I'm not sure if I mean his license or his mind. What I will not know then until

I check the State Bar's website for myself is that the Review Board has already ruled against him. He's deceived me for so long, insisting over and over again that it is still under appeal that he might've even started to believe the lie.

Coincidentally the fax machine goes off in the house, the hub of Liqui-Steal operations inside Psycho Gil's bedroom. It's only too obvious why he always has a cell phone strapped to his shorts. In his irrational need to claim my father's attention, Psycho Gil is probably calling himself.

* * *

"You've only made things worse, Paula," Jim says a week later at the news I've filed a temporary restraining order, written in black ink at the counter of the courthouse. Since finding out he's had to twice go upstairs and pray to his higher power. Our first fight and it's over Holly. Late this afternoon Holly countered, her response typed up by a paralegal. In it, she denies the phone calls, denies tailing me down the Narrows. She claims Jim wants her back. *Miss Priamos is jealous of Mrs. Brown. Filing bogus police reports is the only way she knows how to hold onto a man who simply wants to return to his wife.*

For his part Jim tries to both reassure me about Holly while also getting ready to head off to another A.A. meeting. "She doesn't want to actually hurt you. I mean not physically anyway. She's a good woman. Hol wasn't like this before I left. I'm the one who's done this to her." He holds my shoulders so he'll have my full attention. I've never felt our age difference until right then. "Give her a little more time to get past this."

"Hol, Hol, Hol," I repeat like the child he's treating me. I'm tired of him defending his wife, never me. "Her name has two syllables, not just one."

The two oldest boys are locked away in the bedroom watching TV and the youngest is standing expectantly in the wings in a soggy diaper. He knows the drill and waits while I kneel on the floor and spread newspaper. Jim is too upset about the restraining order to ask why I'm acting as if his child is a puppy that isn't housebroken. Kyle is sensitive to smells, and nearly every time he soils his diaper, he throws up.

Jim waves from behind the screen, torn between his new alliance with me and the more emotionally evident one he still can't quite let go of after nearly twenty years of married life. It's the first time he's ever not kissed me goodbye.

I force myself not to wave back and instead focus on changing Kyle, breaking out the Baby Wipes, the Pampers. The routine swiftness comes back to me from having taken care of Nicholas as a baby. "Countdown, Ky-O," I say as I attach the sticky strips of a fresh diaper, our game that distracts him from the dirty one. "3, 2, 1."

He rolls out fast from the newspaper, all brown eyes and chubby legs, scrambling to his feet. In the months he's been coming over, he knows what comes next.

"Gam Cacker," he hollers, speeding toward the kitchen. The diaper has made him adorably bowlegged.

I follow Kyle in to dispose of the newspaper, the used diaper, and give him a full two squares of his favorite snack that he'll gnaw on for the next half hour.

Suddenly there's a knock on the front screen, and I try to remember if I fastened the tiny hook that anybody, even a three year old, could kick open. The cottage is on a quiet road, a steep one with only one other house above us. Rarely do we get visitors since most of Jim and Holly's friends have taken sides and as the one who's left the marriage, they've chosen the right side, her side.

The knock claps louder, the person behind it becoming more persistent. "Come out, come out," she says. "I know you're in there. My husband just left. *I watched him leave.*"

In the face of the temporary restraining order, she's shown up to confront me. If I were to call the station it would take too long for them to get here, and I realize I've run from this woman for long enough. When I get to the door I'm surprised there isn't more of her. She's petite, barely topping five feet. Her eyes are light brown, slightly bigger than mine, which is where I see Kyle gets the shape of his. The bones in her shoulders show through the work polo she has on with a pair of crisscrossed barbells, the Two-Toned logo, stitched above the right breast. I want to believe she's always been thin and it has nothing to do with the loss of her marriage. Oddly, she's carrying a backpack.

The air crackles, not with tension, but with the sound of Kyle's diaper as he makes his way into the room. At the sight of his mother, he takes a step back, slipping behind my leg. It's as if he knows even at his age she isn't supposed to be here.

Holly's face shows the hurt.

"Say 'hi' to your mom." I reach back and touch Kyle's shoulder, a move that unintentionally sets him further away from his mother.

"Hey, K-Man," she says. For an instant I see what he must see, his mother standing like a prisoner from behind the mesh screen, like someone he should be afraid of. The flimsy hook is unfastened and I think about opening the door, not inviting her in, but at least letting Kyle go outside with her on the porch. My mother's words come back at me, sucker punches from behind. I have cheated this woman out of more than just her husband. I've cheated her of being a mother full time to a little boy still in diapers.

"You think you know everything about him, but you don't," Holly says. "You only know what that no good asshole drunk wants you to know." Her voice and legs are shaky like the ground she's on and the memory of her chasing me down the Narrows catches up with the here and now. With another nudge of her bumper, I could've plunged thousands of feet to my death and it would've looked like an accident, a new resident who didn't know how to handle the roads. She could've gotten into an accident herself, driving that fast with her little boy in the backseat.

"I know enough, Holly," I say. "He's trying to change. If you left him alone, he just might." I've heard it in her voice, how that never would have been a possibility had he stayed in the marriage. There was too much anger, too much damage from his drinking, his affairs. "He has almost ten months' sober time. That's where he's at right now, a meeting."

Something I say pushes Holly into opening the screen, trying to come inside. Her fingernails along the edge of the screen door are chewed down to the pinks.

"You'd better stop right there," I say. I pull back on the screen, only harder, because there is no way I'm letting this woman inside my house.

Sensing trouble, Kyle darts for the stairs, tugging himself up toward the loft where his father and I sleep.

Holly catches her footing on the porch. "It's not too late for you," she whispers. "You can still get out."

At the time I will try and tell myself this threat is just another ploy to get me to leave her husband. Yet I feel she and I might actually be nearing a truce. Soon she will grow exhausted by her own tactics and throw renewed romantic hopes on another man, a quiet, generous real estate developer who takes her on weekend cruises to Catalina Island and Puerta Vallarta. Because she's fallen in love again, in a few years, at forty-four, she will ignore the health risks, the pleas not to go through with it from her oldest son and her former husband, and she will bear this man a beautiful blue-eyed baby girl she names Cassandra. But at her age Holly's body won't prove strong enough to rebound from the physical demands of a difficult pregnancy. Within weeks of bringing a new life into this world, she will inexplicably lose her own from complications detected too late.

When I do think back to the night she showed up at my front door I remember that for a moment she and I understood each other in a way that only two women in love, however madly, with the same man ever could. Jim is the tortured artist and with all that torrent of pain and passion comes a high price. What she lays out for me is not a threat but a warning. If I'm not careful with how much I love him, if I'm not diligent in defining who I am first, I could very well end up like her—my identity so consumed by reacting to his addictive behaviors and unsparing sadness that I turn psychologically troubled myself.

* * *

The next night Jim is over an hour and a half late coming home after teaching and when he does, he's agitated, his face red like he's walked out of a sauna. Without asking, I know he has a half pint of vodka in his book bag.

His ten months are shot with the first swig he probably took out in the parking lot of the liquor store. What he doesn't understand, at least not in his drunken state, is that those ten months were mine too. We constructed them together, day by day, hour by hour, filling them with noon and evening A.A. meetings, the ones that were open to non-drinkers as well, and before dinner trips to the lake to walk off his craving for a drink. I want to cry out over all that time we've just lost. I want to beat the hard tissue of his chest with my fists.

Jim smiles easily and lifts his chin.

"Smells good."

A leg of lamb is reheating, toughening up in the oven.

"It's burnt."

"Don't be mad," he says. "C'mon, Paula. Please lay off. Give me hell tomorrow, just not tonight. Yes, I'm drinking again. I ran into Hol. I mean *Holly*. We got into another fight about money. I don't want to talk about it." He passes me and heads for the kitchen where he turns off the oven. "We can have it for leftovers tomorrow. Come on," he says. "Let's just go."

"Where to?"

"The resort for a drink."

"I won't drink with you."

If I stay home I'm a nag and if I go I'm enabling him.

There is no right decision.

"You won't have to," he says, "I'll order you a Diet Coke."

At the elegant hotel bar with shiny black counter tops he orders a double vodka and a bottle of beer like he did on the plane to Reno. He eyes himself in the mirror behind the bar, then finds me and smiles sheepishly, a self-conscious gesture not in line with how intimate we've become. More is going on than he's willing to reveal. He seems on edge with something the booze can't blunt, and I'm worried he's taken something more than straight alcohol. Maybe he's just concerned he'll run into another one of Holly's friends. Where she works, she's made tons of them, including in the Sheriff's Department where one of them mentioned while I was filling out the form that he'd just seen her when he worked out before coming in for his shift. "I didn't know she was taking the break this hard," he'd said, looking over my report, memorizing the parts he'd probably report back to her.

Jim pulls out a credit card and taps it on the bar, impatiently as if there's something I'm just not getting.

"Okay," he says. "I didn't have a fight with Holly. I made that up because I knew you wouldn't go out with me when I'm drinking. It's getting late," he says, swiveling off the stool. "You have work tomorrow. We should probably go to our room."

"You mean home." What he's saying isn't making sense and I reach in his front pocket for the keys. "You'd better let me drive."

Jim pulls out my hand and playfully tugs me off the stool.

I'm all dead weight, lifeless arms and legs. I don't want to play any more games.

"I mean our room," he says, let down. "Why are you making this so difficult?"

Hand in hand I go along with him as he leads me toward a wing of rooms on the first floor. This is an expensive place, well out of our price range, where the wealthy from Palm Springs and L.A. come for the weekend and enjoy two hundred dollar bottles of wine at lunch and four hundred dollar hot rock massages in the afternoon without breaking a sweat. A one night's stay probably costs half our monthly rent. Jim's hand grips mine tighter, crushing flesh and knuckle, as he stops us in front of one of the room numbers. Getting us here has made him happier than I've ever seen him, not since the bar when I mistook his earlier giddy anxiety for illegal substance abuse.

"You're the right woman for me, Paula," he says. He pauses, bringing my hand he's holding up for a kiss as he descends to one knee. "I know I should tell you that more often. You're pretty, you're tough. You're good to me and my boys . . ."

The rest I'm not really hearing because I can't get past the stunning irony that it's me, the one who tagged along with him to so many A.A. meetings, not his soon to be ex-wife, who is the reason why Jim relapsed. Given his history he knew of no other way to work up the nerve. What I thought was a credit card is an actual hotel card key and when he slips it in the slot and opens the door, I see on the table, next to the chilling bucket of champagne, what Holly as his first wife must've known was coming long before I ever did—a tiny jewelry box wrapped in gold.

* * *

At the news of my engagement I can't tell whether my father is happy for me or if he's simply relieved I've finally gone through with the restraining order. In celebration of one or the other, he invites Jim and me out for dinner at Boca Grande in Chino where my father and I are on a first name basis with Luis, the manager.

"If you're going to marry him after this mess, I suppose it's time I met the *bastardos*." My father is joking when he says this about Jim because he wants to like the only man I've ever moved in with. And I want him to like Jim too.

Over chips and salsa and too many bottles of Dos Equis they will get along yet never come to know each other as father and son-in-law. Not long after their initial meeting that lowlife car jacker in the ski mask is going to emerge from the bushes. He's going to point a gun at my father's side window and threaten to blow his fucking brains out across the front seat. While it first appears my father gets away that night with his life, by morning he won't have gotten away at all.

LIKE MARROW

From the faculty parking lot I hear being announced over and over on the P.A. system that I have a personal phone call. Anybody close to me would use my cell, not the line in the administration office. This is what I know. It is what I fear. In my rush I forget my morning coffee, leaving it on the roof of the car. Whoever is waiting for me wants me in a public place before bearing the bad news. At first I think it's my fiancé who's hurt or worse. He's drinking again and has jammed his BMW against a tree or he's been thrown in jail for a DUI.

"Paula," she says. Lucia is crying too hard for it to be a man she's only met a couple of times. "You need to drive over to my place."

"What's happened?"

"Please, Paula," she says. "Don't ask me that. You need to get over here."

I'm frustrated at her for putting us in a tragic scene straight out of a soap opera.

"How can I when I don't even know *who* it is?"

My emphasis on who prompts the secretary to make a break for the break room. She knows before me too. Lucia's sobbing like I did that afternoon my mother left and I'm afraid of the sound she's making. We've been best friends since the eighth grade. Hurting me doesn't come easily for her.

"Your dad is dead."

The power of those words drain the strength from the backs of my legs and I collapse like one of those Middle Eastern widows seen keening on the evening news over her fallen husband or son—his face or another body part blasted clear off. My purse and contents of my book bag hit the floor too—student essays, grade book, my egg McMuffin from McDonald's I was planning on eating a couple minutes ago. With the receiver in one hand, I can't think of how to clean up my things with the other. I can't think past *my father is dead*.

Efficiency works around me like it would in any office. The secretary, back with a fresh cup of coffee, has already called for a substitute to fill in for me and somebody, a counselor who deals with the difficult cases, is on her knees, patting my back. My pain, not unlike a gravely ill child, is too much even for a professional to watch. The woman looks away from me, wiping her eyes.

"I'll come get you," Lucia says.

Barely listening, I think of another call, my father's from last night at the strip club. Some ghetto thug had pointed a gun at him and now he was dead. Why hadn't I insisted he go to the cops? *Why hadn't I tried harder.* Maybe he would've made it home. I see my father's body doubled over at the wheel. I see his chest and arms spilling out of the car, his head dangling, blood seeping out from the wet hole in his scalp.

I'm about to be sick. I open my eyes so I won't be.

"Was he shot?"

"Shot?

"Did somebody *kill* him."

"No, I think it was a heart attack. Your uncle found him."

She means the man who tried to molest me. There is resentment, there is rage like there always is whenever Psycho Gil is mentioned. I use these hard feelings to hold it together long enough to end the call, to gather my things, find a table and write notes to my sub. None of what I've just heard adds up yet I find some purpose in laying out what I do know, the lesson plans my students will follow in my absence. Five days' paid leave is how much time I'll receive to mourn the man I've spent nearly thirty years of my life loving.

* * *

Uncle Dimitri is in a hurry to bury my father. He's made this no secret. Inside of a couple hours, with my father's body still at the coroner's office, he's set up an appointment at the funeral home. Chapel of Remembrance is a few exits down from Yia Yia's house, off the 91 freeway in Artesia, the same city where Bared Garratta bought the gun he blew away his boss with. We've taken Uncle Dimitri's car with Yia Yia, Jim and me in the backseat. My fiancé has tried to calm me, not just with words of comfort or his arm clamped around my shoulders, but with Valium that he pushed on me when he picked me up at Lucia's apartment. As someone who has relied on drugs to numb himself from deep emotional pain, he can't stand to see mine raw and at the surface. I have him worried. Grief has given me a tolerance unknown to a lightweight. My body has so far fought off two of the powerful little pills. In order to tend to my needs Jim has gone stone cold sober.

Psycho Gil remains at the house to field calls and stay away from me. I have questions. Because he isn't here, I direct them at Yia Yia. As the only other person in the house when my father was found, she knows things. Like what was Psycho Gil doing in my father's room before dawn? Did my father make a noise? Was he in pain? How long had he lain there dying? Was it his heart or an attack of another kind? Yia Yia wouldn't know. Presumably out of concern for her well being, by the time she reached the room her son's body was covered in a sheet. She lets it slip that even more time passed between Psycho Gil finding my father dead and when one of them dialed 911. Coffee was made and the two of them got dressed.

"Gil didn't see the rush. He said your father was cold to the touch," she explains as if this makes perfect sense.

"Did he even *try* and revive him?"

What I say or maybe how I say it causes Jim to take his arm off my shoulders and pull out another tiny pill from the tin foil in his pocket.

"Take it dry," he says in my ear. "Please, Baby. Have another one for me."

"It's a *simple question*," I say to Jim and everybody else in the car who have all grown quiet.

"Paula, Paula," Uncle Dimitri cuts in. "None of that's important now. Let's just take care of one thing at a time."

When it comes to Psycho Gil Uncle Dimitri is no different from the rest of the family. If anything he's worse. Uncle Dimitri sees his brother Gil as a genetic embarrassment, a reflection of their own convoluted gene pool. This includes not just Uncle Dimitri, but his four perfect sons, all of whom he'd go to any lengths to protect.

Yia Yia chomps around on dentures she forgot to glue down. They make a loose clackety noise. No matter what I think she might be leaving out, I back off. She's unhinged. I can see that. I squeeze strength into her bony hand. In less than one day she's lost that too.

Lola rides in the front. Since moving in with Uncle Dimitri, she's quit her job serving drinks and now serves only him from answering the phones at the office, to riding with him to the track after hours. They're inseparable.

"This is your call, Paula," Uncle Dimitri declares, his eyes on the next exit. He triggers the blinker. After getting in the BMW with him I've noticed a careful detachment about his brother's death and I guess for him there is no other way. "Pick out whatever casket and flowers you see fit. You're Paul's next of kin, even before your brother and sister. We all know that."

"That's right," pipes in Lola. She's dabbing on lip gloss in the visor mirror. "The two of you were like a little team."

The Valium must finally be taking effect because there is no other explanation why I find some consolation in an outsider like Lola being able to pin down in one line the complicated relationship between me and my father.

* * *

Inside Chapel of Remembrance, the director approaches Uncle Dimitri first. He's been expecting us, and I'm curious if the two of them have already met in court or at the track. Anyone who knows Uncle Dimitri understands he's too impatient to be kept waiting. Antonio Sanchez is a squat man with dark eyes set close to his nose and a tie that's too short and points midway at his boulder belly.

This is family business, blood business. No matter how much

Uncle Dimitri may have fallen for Lola, she's left to wait in the lobby with my fiancé. As if to get us back or maybe because cocktail hour is nearing and old habits die hard, she sits close to Jim, talking even closer.

After getting settled in Mr. Sanchez's office he hands me a photo album filled with caskets. Pine. Birch. Cherry wood. Bland white roses or orchids drape over them and lean arranged on easels. In one picture dark red roses are strangled like seaweed at the foot of the coffin. In another the flowers are bright and festive and come with complimentary balloons.

"That one there is a real show piece," Mr. Sanchez says, nodding in approval.

Without realizing it I've paused on a purple lamé casket with glittery silver fixtures and dyed lilac chrysanthemums to match. I turn the page, turning on Mr. Sanchez just as fast.

"My father's a lawyer, not a pimp."

Uncle Dimitri chuckles it off and then Mr. Sanchez does too. But I wasn't meaning to be funny. I wasn't meaning anything. There is none anymore. Even with my fiancé waiting for me down the hall, with family on either side of me, I feel abandoned. I loved my father more than any of them.

"There should be an obituary in *The Times*," Yia Yia shouts. She glances around to make sure someone's heard her. Jim and Lola probably did from down the hall. In the chaos of her son dying, Yia Yia has also neglected to insert her hearing aid.

"Sure, Mom," Uncle Dimitri says loudly. He leans toward me in case Yia Yia can read lips. "You understand, Paula, why I can't let that happen. Over the years your father made more enemies than he ever had clients. There will be no obituary. It's bad enough word might leak out before he's in the ground."

I nod, wishing he'd stop speaking of something that should go without saying. Halfway through the album I settle on a dark grain casket with silver gauge fixtures. I can't remember what color the lining is but I remember the color of the flowers. They're yellow roses, only yellow. Yellow is the color of jealousy, which my father carried in his bones like marrow once he learned my mother started a new life with another man. It's also the color of my brother's old room in Chino that my father had spent all day painting. Nick and Rhea are flying in tomorrow morning.

Burying the dead doesn't come cheap—approximately it's the cost of a small Hyundai. Uncle Dimitri pulls out his platinum credit card to pay for the casket, the flowers, the preparation of my father's body, the two motor escorts. Uncle Dimitri makes a point of ordering two limousines, perhaps anticipating family friction, especially between me and Psycho Gil. When the director returns after having left the room to discreetly make sure Uncle Dimitri's credit card is good, he hands over the contract to Uncle Dimitri who then passes it to me.

Mr. Sanchez shakes hands again with Uncle Dimitri, finalizing things.

"The funeral is set for tomorrow afternoon at four, Mr. Priamos."

"Tomorrow?" I stop reading things over. "His body is here *now?*" This part I don't understand. What strings Uncle Dimitri had to pull in order to execute a funeral in under twenty-four hours. Clearly he's doing more than simply burying his brother. He's covering something up. My brother and sister's plane could be late or in their emotional state of mind they could miss it altogether. Not to mention this is Southern California. We will hit traffic. "So there's already been an autopsy."

Uncle Dimitri grimaces and waves me off as if I've requested something as outrageous as my father's head to be lopped off and frozen in a Cryonics chamber.

"There's no point in any of that, Paula. They cost too much and besides, he's dead. Cracking his chest open isn't going to bring him back."

What Uncle Dimitri says floors me with more than its coldness. My father had just been to see the doctor. His blood pressure was in check. I don't believe Uncle Dimitri then nor do I know the reasons he was against an autopsy. Odds are he knows people in the coroner's office just like he does everybody in the Los Angeles County court system and if pressed they would easily grant him such a request.

* * *

The funeral gets pushed back one precious day so my sister and brother have time to fly in. I pick them up the next morning in Ontario, the halfway point between my house in the mountains and Yia Yia's. They've flown in on the red eye. My sister's eyes are bloodshot which has little to do with traveling all night. All in black, so are Rhea's tears from her mascara. Nicholas, nearly six feet of him, supports her. Her meds have let her down. A crowd collects behind them, passengers anxious to get around this woman, humped over in heartache, that's holding them up. She is also without her little girl, her lifeline. After much consideration, not to mention a call from Yia Yia stating that as the ex-wife she has no place at a Priamos family funeral, my mother thinks it best she stay behind in Tennessee with Annabelle. "The divorce isn't why she doesn't want me there." My mother's voice cracks with loss. She's been widowed without the legal rights to even call it that. "Your yia yia's protecting the wrong son again. She knows Gil can't handle being in the same room with me, especially now that your father isn't here to stand between us."

At the airport my brother looks surprisingly put together the way I will learn in times of crisis he will always appear. He's wearing a John Deere green and yellow cap, the bill smudged with dirt. From underneath he catches my eyes, then rolls his. He was a baby when our sister tried to end her own life. It's better he thinks she's being melodramatic and isn't experiencing a mental breakdown right in front of him. His smile is measured, maybe to wait and see if I will return it. I'm not sure if I do. I haven't slept or eaten in over twenty-four hours.

"Hey, Sis."

"Nicholoso."

I hug him first because he needs it, a high school junior having shepherded our grief-stricken older sister nearly two thousand miles on his own.

"Oh, Paula," Rhea mutters. She's crying in a quiet, damaged way.

In frustration but also in an attempt to lift her spirits, Nicholas rips off his cap and rubs at his hair that's as dense and unmovable as Astroturf and says, "Goddamn, Rhea. Enough with the water works." He fits the cap back on again. "I'm surprised ya'll got any more tears left in those puffy ol' eyes of yours."

I take over for my brother, and I put my arm around Rhea's shoulders, guiding her out of the terminal and to my car. Late spring feels like summer and neither one of them, she in a sweater and long skirt, he in a sweatshirt and jeans, are prepared for the dry desert heat. To help Rhea feel more at home, we stop at a drive-thru. I order her a forty-four ounce Diet Coke. From the backseat, Nicholas pushes in between us, not wanting to be left out.

"I just keep thinkin' back to why Uncle Gil was in Dad's room in the first place. Hell, at that hour, I mean it was earlier than the chickens even think to roost."

"I don't know," I say and I don't. There is no point in fueling his suspicions with the fact Psycho Gil was left alone in the bedroom with our father's body for any amount of time before calling for help. We're on our way to the house now. In order to feel closer to him, both Rhea and Nicholas want to see for themselves our father's room.

Yia Yia responds to seeing her estranged granddaughter utterly destroyed at her front door by taking Rhea in her arms, welcoming her weakness. It only reaffirms Yia Yia's talk that my sister is emotionally unstable. Psycho Gil is seated in a rocking chair, watching the financial news in his Ocean Pacific beach wear and slippers. He keeps his eyes on the screen, refusing to look at the three of us. I've seen that kind of focus before, years before, when he received the letter in his little girl's scrawl that she never wanted to see him again. He's about ready to blow.

The first thing I notice in my father's room are the flat moving boxes stacked against the closet door that have yet to be assembled. Either my father was planning to move out or within one day of finding him dead, Yia Yia and Psycho Gil already have plans of storing away his belongings. The air smells of coconuts. Psycho Gil has recently been in here.

Rhea cries inconsolably at the shrine of photographs our father made for his granddaughter on the wall. He may never have flown out to see her but he put up every picture Rhea ever sent him. She snatches one—a picture of Annabelle as a baby in a pumpkin orange jumper during Halloween. Rhea couldn't help herself and drew little lipstick hearts on her daughter's plump cheeks.

"I didn't know," she keeps saying over and over, sinking into more than just the black leather couch which folds out to a bed. She's gone to a place in her mind I will have to call my mother to figure out how to reach.

An old jalopy air conditioner blocks the window, the only other way into the room if someone didn't want to be caught coming in through the bedroom door. On the night stand is a glass with an inch or two of what looks like water. I pick it up and inhale the sweet smelling ouzo—a party drink not meant to be consumed in a bedroom all alone. What slight solace I do find is in what I haven't found. No empty prescription bottle of pills. No weepy note filled with regret or goodbyes. To an outsider, things were looking better for my father. He'd passed the CBEST and just started subbing. Now that he was earning an income again there were plans to get his own apartment, to send out applications and teach business classes part-time at a community college.

While the thought of earning his first paycheck temporarily picked him up, I'd heard it in his voice how the upcoming anniversary of his disbarment was getting to him. Earning a hundred and five dollars a day following the lesson plans of another instructor is a far cry from arguing in front of a judge and jury on behalf of an alleged rapist or murderer with a six figure retainer in the bank.

Any traces of an overdose Yia Yia, I realize, would've gotten rid of, which might explain why Psycho Gil held off on calling for help. Yia Yia has plans to hold the services at St. John the Baptist's in Anaheim or Saint Sophia's in Los Angeles where my parents were married. Yia Yia attends both because sometimes, she says, she grows tired of hearing the same gossip. The Greek Orthodox Church doesn't condone suicide.

Someone who takes his own life goes to hell. If my father has in fact killed himself, the church will refuse his body for services.

Underneath the nightstand I spot his cell phone that must've fallen in the commotion yesterday morning. I grab it and retrieve his voice mail.

One call is from my brother telling him about the mess of trout he caught on a trip to the Mississippi River with friends. Although nearly two weeks old I imagine my father played it back countless times just to hear his son's voice.

The next call is trash. Street talk and cursing.

Some enraged gang banger with nothing to lose. It's not about money owed. It's not that kind of call. My father is a motherfucker. Threats are shouted and will be carried out if he doesn't return the call. No number and for that matter no name is left as if my father should already know. Technically, after the initial shock wears off, after I replay the message a couple times I hear it for what it is—an angry rant. Another person my father has pushed too far. Like Beth Anne's ex-husband, a once respectable businessman, whose fury toward my father knew no bounds when he staked out our home, then vandalized it in the middle of the night.

The difference between them is that this man can't possibly be a former client. He sounds capable of much more than a horseshoe flung through the bedroom window. He sounds capable of donning a ski mask and gloves and swearing he'll blow a man's brains out. He sounds capable of murder. My head pulsates with what I now know. I feel like I need air, more than that suffocatingly small room rank with liquor and suntan oil can provide. The phone is like lead in my hand. I don't want to keep to myself what might be the identity of my father's killer or at least the sound of his voice. *But my father died here in his sleep.*

"Rhea." I turn to her. "You need to hear this."

On the couch with her daughter's picture in her lap my sister can't seem to hear me.

The message was left two days ago, the day before the almost carjacking. This is too much of a coincidence—a set-up that backfired. Nobody factored in my father's Greek temper, his split-second refusal to play the role of the middle-aged white male victim.

"You were no kind of son to your father." The words are unmistakably clear even though they've come from down the hall in the living room where I never should have left my brother. The exchange is quick and cutting, the way the Priamos family has always been with each other when something goes terribly wrong.

Before I have a chance to come out, my brother is already heading through the doorway.

"That crazy son of a bitch." Nicholas is crying, he is cursing. The hurt behind his words is significant.

Psycho Gil is not far behind, armed with the cordless. The other hand is stashed in the front pocket of his shorts. Yet I'm not as scared as I should be of the small handgun I know he's fingering. He wouldn't shoot us in broad daylight, not with the stoner boys home next door. The blond one is out in the driveway washing their VW bug.

Psycho Gil leans in mere inches from my brother's face.

"I'm calling the cops and having you arrested."

I step in front of Nicholas because he's only a boy of sixteen. Both a coward and a bully, Psycho Gil is an unpredictable and violent man. There is no doubt as to which one of us is the looser cannon. I am reckless in my grief. What I'm about to say is not just for the thirteen year old who used her head and locked herself in the bathroom, frantically dialing her parents in the hopes they'd be able to somehow stop this monster from two thousand miles away. It's not just for my sister who was sexually violated in a place where she too should've felt safe, her father's very own law office. It's also for my mother who endured the harassment, the inappropriate comments and stares for so long, throughout her entire marriage. This does not, however, justify her abrupt dismissal in my cry for help that night. No parent should ever ignore the innocent pleas of her child.

"Do it," I dare Psycho Gil. "Call the cops and I'll tell them how you tried to *fuck* me and my sister."

Still crying in some kind of catatonic state, Rhea provides little in the form of back-up. Clearly she doesn't need to. My threat is enough to strike real fear in Psycho Gil's eyes and he drops the phone to his side, the closest he'll ever come to an admission of guilt.

"Shut up," he says. "*Just shut up.*"

What happens next is a blur, me running for the front door. On the TV screen the ticker tape below reels the numbers of the Nasdaq, the Dow Jones. The door is slammed behind me. I hear the slide and click of the dead bolt. Outside on the front lawn, it's eerily quiet. This is how some tragedies play out, in the bright sunlight during the middle of the day in a pleasant housing tract like this one. An entire family gets wiped out, each with a clean shot in the head execution style, usually by one man, a father, a husband, or in this case a younger brother, who in his despair at all that he's lost, no longer recognizes the importance of life anymore. I scream for my brother and sister who are now locked inside the house with him. My chest throbs with what I expect to hear next, the sound of gun shots, then silence. I've pushed him to the breaking point. I don't have much time.

The stoner boys, as Psycho Gil's neighbors, must know it too. Both of them are in their driveway, barefoot, sudsing up the car. They must've heard the fighting, Psycho Gil's voice escalating minutes earlier inside the house. They must've witnessed his insane behavior countless times before because when I tell them that my sister and brother are still locked in the house with my uncle, neither one hesitates. The dark haired one is shirtless, lean and muscled. They are probably more sober than I am, given the heavy dose of Valium Jim has kept me on for the past twenty-four hours. The blond with the shaggy hair lets go of the hose, leaving the water draining down the driveway. He pounds on Yia Yia's front door with his brother not far behind.

"Hey, Gil," he yells. "Open up before there's any more trouble. Your niece wants her brother and sister out here *now*."

With my father gone he might see taking his own life as the next logical step. Psycho Gil has no one to live for anymore. He has no one to share his dream of becoming a billionaire recluse like his hero Howard Hughes. He has no one to ride out the long days with, to stuff his pipe and smoke it out on the patio with and leaf through *World Aircraft* magazine, pointing out the type of luxury private plane he'll one day purchase, no one to walk the park with, no one to dream through those close phone calls and faxes that haven't quite panned out yet, about the millions Liqui-Steal will eventually generate if only the FBI would just back off.

The dark haired neighbor rattles the knob. He throws his shoulder into the door. One of them turns to me and mentions we might need to call the cops.

I am only half listening. Part of me keeps waiting for the gun shots.

225

Then the blond hoists his leg about to kick in the door when Yia Yia finally appears. Her arm is around my sister who, in her distress and dark clothes, is serving as the white flag, the reason why nobody came to the door for all this time. Comforting a granddaughter whom she has openly called for years a nutcase and a liar shows just how far the old woman is willing to go to protect her own disturbed son. Psycho Gil stands the way he always does, not far behind her, having once again, with her help, gained a false sense of balance.

"You think I'm hiding something?" he says. "Go ahead, Paula. Why don't you write about it."

* * *

At the funeral I look for her. I look for Sugar Brown. Although I've never seen her in person, I know I'll recognize her when I do. If she cared at all, if she has nothing to hide, she'll be here. In my purse is my father's cell. I have a message I want to play back for her.

The only woman close to my age inside the church who does meet my gaze with me is Sarafina, a distant relative. It's a good thing she's seated clear on the other side of the church when she gives me a sad, pouty face like I'm a child who's lost my favorite toy, not a parent. At thirty-one, she's already on her second husband. She's also going on her second pair of breasts. They were flown in from Milan, a rumored wedding gift from her rich businessman husband who claimed he wanted the two of them to start fresh and preferred not touching her smaller natural set another man had already fondled.

The church is lopsided with people like a wedding with the bride and groom's families taking up their respective side of the church. The

Greeks show unity behind Yia Yia and Psycho Gil. There is no telling what the two of them told the rest of the relatives and I can't say I care anymore. None of the family bothers to hear our side. None of them even ask.

Absent of my mother and Annabelle all the family I need is here in the first pew with me—my brother, my sister, Lucia, and Jim whom I'm about to marry this summer on the Tahoe shore. He's been my rock, my muscle since my father's death and I love him all the more for it. After hearing what happened at Yia Yia's yesterday afternoon Jim and his foul mouth refuse to leave my side. "I know I have my share of problems, but I love you," he tells me on the ride to the church, "and I can promise you one thing. Nobody in that fucked up family of yours will *ever* hurt you again."

The stoner boys and their mother find a place a few rows behind us. The blond who came to help first lifts his hand, not exactly a wave but something close to it. What looks like a bandage is wound tightly up to his wrist, the results of having banged so hard on Yia Yia's front door.

I will be the last of the mourners to pass by my father's open casket to say my final goodbyes. He will be dressed in a suit like the lawyer he used to be yet he looks nothing like himself. His face appears windblown and if he bears any injuries they're smoothed and hidden beneath all that orange make-up. His thick wavy hair, thinning at the temples, the hair that he washed his entire life with a bar of soap, is parted on the wrong side. When I touch his chest it's hollow and deceptively hard like a fragile shell that might cave if I'm not careful.

My oldest cousin William watches me from the side of the church like a curious driver who's come across a fatal car accident. He can't help himself. As one of the pall bearers he seems at once both fascinated and impatient why I'm holding things up, why I'm still standing over my father's body, fingering the ruffled edge of the coffin, unable to let go. His love for his own father is controlled, it's practical. He's been a middle-aged man since he was a teenager. At sixteen his father offered to buy him whatever car he wanted. Instead of a Porsche or a Mustang, William chose a brand new, boxy, four door Volvo.

I slip a silver dollar in my father's shirt pocket taken from the jar topped full of them I still keep on my dresser, our days diving for dollars. Reassurance is what I need that a piece of me, a piece of the two of us, is buried with him. As my father he has always been a biological part of me, in my blood, my bones, my laughter. He is the darkness in my eyes, and I weep for the man who isn't there. I weep for having to remember him here like this, groomed by a stranger's hands. I loosen his tie. I correct his part.

She is not here. Sugar Brown is a no show. The time the two of them spent, at least for her, hadn't meant more than a cash transaction. He was her john, and she was his whore, and it is right then as I'm saying goodbye to my father that I make him a promise. If that woman doesn't have enough decency to show her face here, I will catch up to her while she's in the act at the strip club.

LATE SHOWING

The deadly coincidences that occurred during my father's final hours are no more believable now than when I was first told about them. Like a vivid and violent nightmare, the mystery of that night afflicts me unexpectedly, stopping me in the middle of lecturing to my class, while I'm fixing dinner, or when I'm lying in bed waiting for sleep. As a defense attorney my father insisted I always look at something from all angles and if it doesn't add up, I need to figure out why. If I apply that to our last conversation when he called from the strip club, then I can only come to the unsettling conclusion that he knew he wasn't going to make it. It's why he had me promise I would finish school and become a professor before I ever thought of being a mother. He sensed he wouldn't be around to look after me. Maybe the physical symptoms had already started—the shortness of breath and fatigue. Maybe he was hoping against hope that if he took a few extra blood pressure pills when he got back to Yia Yia's he might sleep off the trauma of having nearly just lost his life. The final lesson he would teach the daughter who stood by him after the break-up of the family is perhaps one of the most important he ever taught me. It's not so much that he didn't want me to completely love Jim and start our own family, but rather that I remember to fulfill my dreams and goals along the way.

Despite my brother and sister somehow coming to terms with our father's death without having all the answers, I can't let it go so easily. At the Compton police station where I ask for help I wind up being questioned myself by the irritated officer working the front desk, as if I am the one with something to hide. He seems to think it wasn't loneliness that led a man as educated as my father to the ghetto. My father must've been a crack head.

Frustrated, I decide to wait for hours if need be outside in the parking lot at the Kat Nip in Garden Grove. I wait for her, Sugar Brown, because when I asked around inside I got nowhere. The stucco building is two stories, painted hot pink, with a neon sign promising TONS OF SWEET FELINES AND TWO WILDCATS. The same figure of a sexy cat woman kicking up a stiletto that I found on the match book in my father's pocket stretches up part of the sign.

I should've known better than to try and bribe anybody in the kind of seedy place that operates off illusion, paying for what you'll never actually get, whether it's sex or answers. The only person who provides me with any credible information is the bartender who clams up once his boss comes by. The owner is a disturbingly tall man in his early thirties with an expensive suit and a pencil tucked behind one ear. His talk is articulate and British. A cleaned up Eurotrash pimp. I wouldn't be surprised if he holds a bachelor's degree in business from either UCLA or USC. It definitely comes as no real shock when after pressing him about Sugar, he claims he has no idea who I'm talking about and in the politest means possible, escorts me to the exit.

During the time I've been sitting in my car I've drunk two large cups of bad coffee from an all night donut shop down the street. In this part of town there are no Starbucks. Besides it's getting late. At half past midnight, where things inside the club are just starting to heat up, my time has run out. Jim thinks I'm at the movies with Lucia. Even if it's a late showing I should be home by now. Twice he's tried calling my cell. Trust doesn't come easily for him and I'm betraying his by not telling him the truth about where my suspicions have taken me. He's told me repeatedly to just let it go. My father died of a heart attack. So what if there was no autopsy. Look at the facts, he tells me. My pappou died from it and Uncle Dimitri nearly did too.

But if I am to believe Jim then I'm to believe the young stripper my father saw that night, with whom he deluded himself into thinking they had a real, bonafide relationship, bears no responsibility in his death. And I cannot accept that. I won't. I don't buy that she didn't know a gunman would be jumping out of the bushes, threatening to murder my father. The fact that no shots were fired is of little consequence. Whether it was from an actual gun shot or a heart attack brought on hours later by the lingering terror of having a gun pointed at his head, my father still died that night.

Like I expect, a young black woman soon comes out of the club. She glances around the lot, not looking too worried. I left nearly an hour before, long enough for her to think the coast is clear. Comfortable in sweats, a tight tank, and flip flops, her hair is just as casual, hidden in a Dodger's baseball cap. Her body is curvy yet taut from hours working the pole. Animatedly she chats on her cell, joking possibly to her boyfriend, the one that held a gun to my father's head.

She's letting him in on how she outsmarted the daughter of one of her johns, you know, the one that caused them all the problems, the one that's now six feet under. She's probably telling him how I came in asking questions, how she hid in the back, in another dressing room or in the boss's office while her girl Erica, had her back. She's probably telling him how after I was given the runaround, they both then split my money. Nearly two day's worth of teaching that for Sugar and Erica would probably take less than one dance to collect in their g-strings. Sugar throws her head back, laughing, as she clicks off her car alarm. Apparently her tips pay off because she gets into a shiny Mustang, a new one with no plates.

I follow her out of the lot, make another quick turn onto Garden Grove Boulevard, and soon we're getting on the 22 where it connects to the 405 toward Santa Monica, then on to the 710. My nerves are jumpy from all the coffee, from the fact I'm two car lengths away from Sugar Brown, the girl my father went to see nearly every night, either to watch her dance or take her out afterward, the girl he tried so hard to keep from me. I know it's her. We're heading in the right direction, past the scrap metal junk yards on the outskirts of Long Beach. We pass the graffiti streaked exits for Lynwood, the ones for Compton too, until she finally sets her blinker on the turn-off for Firestone Boulevard in South Gate.

This nearly stops me. It's just one city over. Still, Uncle Dimitri had told me Compton. Because he grew up in this area he wouldn't make the mistake of mixing up the two cities. On one corner is a Pop-eye's chicken fast food restaurant, a strip mall with bars across all the windows—a Coin-Op laundry, a check cashing store. A man in a flannel shirt and jeans lies motionless on his side in the parking lot. I'm not sure if he's unconscious from a mugging or if he's simply a drunk passed out in an unlikely place.

Sugar makes a quick stop at a 7-Eleven when my cell goes off again. Looking back at my actions that night I can see that I was spiraling out of control with my grief, my suspicions. I'd become a hazard not just to myself but to her, the young stripper I couldn't stop following.

This time I pick up.

"Where are you?" Sober and back in A.A. meetings since my father's death, Jim sounds more concerned than angry, the step by step principles of the program he follows at work. These past couple weeks he says, in the kindest way possible, I haven't been acting like myself. He's even made an appointment for me to see a psychologist.

"My car battery died," I say.

Sugar is now in the refrigerated section, pulling out a half gallon of thick milk, a dozen eggs. A little light grocery shopping in an all night convenience store.

"Why didn't you call?" he says.

"I didn't want to make you drive all the way down here." The lie is getting easier, sounding more plausible. Sugar is at the counter paying for her food. I lean across the dash. At some point she also picked up a six pack of beer. "Somebody in the parking lot had some jumper cables," I continue.

"You're sure that's all it is?" Jim senses I'm somewhere I shouldn't be.

An elderly black man in mechanics coveralls holds open the door for Sugar as she exits the store, carrying two bags. I'm close enough to see her mouth a thank you with those plump pin cushion lips my father probably paid extra to kiss.

"Yes, I'm sure," I say. "I'm on my way home now."

"I hope so, Paula," he says, before hanging up. "You know, you and me, we have a good thing up here."

He loves me and has given up so much for us to be together that I imagine, at times like this when I test his trust, he can't help but question if he's made the right choice. But there is no time for me to patiently explain that I'm not out cheating with some other guy because Sugar is on the move again.

The housing tract where she lives is no ghetto. Naturally, given the city limits, there are bars on the front windows and doors, but the houses are old sixties style with flat rooftops, flower gardens and neatly mowed lawns. As she pulls into the driveway of a pale colored one story with dark trim, a light fills up one of the front rooms. Within seconds the curtains part and a little boy knocks on the glass. He can't be more than Kyle's age, probably younger, three, tops.

"What're you doin' up, little big man?" Sugar says. She's out of the car, handling the bags. "Get yourself back into bed." Her voice is different, softer even in reprimand, than it was earlier when she was on her cell.

The affection in it, even with my car windows closed, carries all the way across the street where I am parked.

It never occurred to me that my father's Sugar had a domestic life of potty training and whole milk. I pictured her as the hard partying type in some all night dope house the cops continuously came by and busted. Things are not as black and white as I need them to be.

Disobeying her, the little boy flings open the front door. The sensor triggers the porch light, and I see he's wearing baggy Spider Man pajamas, the kind with feet.

"Mommy!" The boy reaches out to be picked up. His head, like his pajamas, is too big for his body. "What kind of candy did you bring me?"

My father would've enjoyed coming here and playing with her little boy genius who at his young age perfectly sounds out a phonetically correct and complex sentence. Maybe, before and after, my father sat Sugar's son on his lap and helped the little boy with his vowels. I am confused at my anguish in seeing that this woman offered him something far more substantial than just sex. My father was good with kids and missed out on most of his own son's years spent in action hero pajamas.

Instinctively the girl turns the way people do when they know they're being watched—a little cautious, even more vulnerable.

My breath is gone, my hands gripped in position at ten and two at the wheel where I've been braced to make a quick getaway ever since I got here. She's looking directly at me. I reassure myself that's not possible. Parked several feet from any street lamps, all she must see is the make and color of my car. I doubt if my father even told her that much about me. Her eyes stay on my car as she nudges her son into the house. In her neighborhood she must be used to being on constant guard. I could use her fear to my advantage and jump out now and cross the street. I could briefly introduce myself and ask her point blank if she had anything to do with what happened to my father because the truth is I don't know. I don't even know for sure if I've followed the right girl.

Years later during a visit to my sister's home outside Knoxville, Tennessee, she will finally reveal to me what our father told her, that Sugar Brown watched like this girl is doing right now from the front door of her home while somebody in a ski mask and gloves came toward the loud running Mercedes, my father sitting like a lame duck in the driver's seat. The girl never calls for help. As a gun is aimed at my father's head, she deliberately locks eyes with him. In that one heartless stare she does more to finish him off than my mother ever did by her insensitive move more than halfway across the country with their young son.

Why Rhea waits so long to tell me, I'm not sure except that in some way I'd like to think she was protecting me from what I might've done right then outside that stripper girl's house had I known the truth. My father didn't want me finding out about this part of his life, the hard, unlawful streets he chose to come back to after losing it all. Out of shame or secrecy, the reason doesn't matter anymore. Coming here, being with a woman like Sugar, might've been all my father was capable of. The love of his life since high school, the good decent mother of his children, whom he wrote nonstop letters to in an attempt to win back, no longer cared. So why not pay for the intimacy up front. The feeling couldn't be much different than how his ex-wife now treated him.

Sugar's gaze does not falter, and I am aware of the immediate trouble I may be in. She is only seconds away from calling whoever has been inside the house all this time babysitting her child, the person for whom she bought the Colt 45.

My car idles because I've forgotten to turn off the engine. I crank the wheel and gun the gas, and I drive, just drive right past this dumbfounded stripper girl and her house, past the boulevard with the bars on all the store windows, the hookers in high heels and short shorts that have already taken to the sidewalks, the man still sprawled out in the parking lot.

He could be dead.

I take the shortest cuts, connecting to the different numbered freeways that I never formerly memorized by name but that I know as a native by heart. I pass Lakewood where I've recently learned Yia Yia and Psycho Gil are busily packing up because either my words that afternoon in my father's room or my father having died in there have left them wanting to clear out all the way to another state. I pass Rose Hills where my father is newly buried, not far from my pappou. I pass the slopes of Diamond Bar, the high school where I work, its tin roof reflecting like glass in the moonlight. I pass the Central Avenue exit for Chino that's always meant my home though not any longer. I pass the Ontario Airport, the flickering underbelly of a departing plane. As soon as I get off the right exit and start up the twenty mile incline to the home where my fiancé is worried and waiting for me, I decide to keep from him the darker places I've been tonight. For now, at least, I am five thousand feet above it all in the San Bernardino Mountains.

CASELOAD

My father doesn't leave a will but he does leave behind a hefty monthly bill for me to pay at Sailor Sam's Storage Facility located under a freeway overpass in Montclair. The unit he rented is packed floor to ceiling with furniture and random belongings from the Chino house and his office. The truth is that I've been putting off clearing it out for months, but with steep alimony payments money is tight and Jim and I can no longer afford me to.

I rely on my fiancé's physical strength to help me as well as his experience having done this once already after his brother shot himself. He takes only a few things, an old jacket, some of the favorite books they shared. The pillow, squirming underneath with maggots, where his brother last laid his head—that he left behind. Jim has been sober now since my father's death and last week I was with him when he received his three month chip at a meeting.

One weekend not long before the wedding, Jim rents a U-Haul truck and takes his oldest son, Alan, with him to remove everything from the unit. Lucia borrows her father's Ford Ranger pick-up. Her hair is pulled back in that old snood she used to wear. She means business as do I with mine held up off my neck with a rubber band. I'm in a black T-shirt and cut-off shorts to hide the dirt. The two of us are in charge of another kind of heavy lifting—disposing of all of my father's legal files—over two decades worth of failed marriages, new business partnerships, individuals exonerated of crimes as well as current inmates of the California state prison system. Because the metal file cabinets are stored all the way in the back of the unit I haven't been able to get to them and count just how many there are.

Piece by piece Jim and his son take away the remnants of my father's life, like the wall painting of a trail leading from a thatched roof cottage into the forest that used to hang in the foyer of the Chino house. It was one of the rare items my mother had flagged with a Post-It and the movers had missed.

"Hold on," I call out to Alan. I'm halfway to the filing cabinets as I reverse my way back, banging up my knees and calves along the way. He slides up the back door and I pull out that ugly Hansel and Gretel painting. Carefully I lean the gold-flecked frame against the wall of the unit designated for the items I'm keeping, like my father's old Rolodex with his clients' contact information.

Of the phone numbers I'll gather I will decide on only two of his former clients to call—one a killer, the other a crook who, if I'm to believe my father, cheated him out of a fortune in grove profits. I'm not sure why I want to talk to them except that I'm hopeful I'll hear real sorrow or remorse in their voices upon breaking the news that the lawyer who spared them from life behind bars is now dead.

With what seems like no time and no real dent made in the unit, a first load in the U-Haul is ready to go. Fortunately, Jim finds a Goodwill store just down the street. He starts up the engine, then hops out from behind the wheel.

"We'll be back in a few minutes." He kisses my forehead, patting my back with a thick leather glove. "This will all be over soon, Baby."

His freckle-faced fifteen-year-old son, on the other hand, doesn't look so optimistic. He strains his neck at what's left in the unit as if it's a sky scraper he's expected to scale.

Lucia gives me a leg up and I cross atop the geography of my father's and my life—the refrigerator and freezer where my father used to keep the bottles of ouzo from Lesvos, the professional portraits of Pride's Contract and Midnight's Secret Wish, the show horses he lost to either old age or Rhea's former lover Dumbo, and the tan leather love seat worn at the arms from where my father rested his while he channel surfed and where I used to sprawl out across the length of it and watch TV as he pored drunkenly through family slides. Even with the door to the unit open, the air inside is dusty and hot, and I have to wipe my forehead with the tail of my tank to clear the perspiration from my eyes.

Lucia shines a beam from a flashlight in my eyes.

"Well?" she says expectantly. "How many?"

It takes me twice to count them all.

"Eighteen."

"Eighteen?"

"Yeah," I say again, "eighteen."

"Mother of God."

Lucia is trying to curb her cursing. At nearly thirty she's dashed all hopes of ever making it as an actress and now teaches Kindergarten at a private Catholic school.

The protocol for what to do with a deceased, disbarred lawyer's files is lost on me. His former clients should've asked for their files back once they learned his license had been revoked. All the necessary documents, I figure, are on file with the court anyway.

I begin with the business partnerships, pulling out by the arm load bulging manila files, the papers punctured with a two-hole punch, held down between the covers with metal brackets. The Fly Bye owners hired my father for a partnership with a Japanese businessman when they decided to open up a second restaurant in Chino Hills. They now own close to ten nearby airports all across the Pacific Northwest. In one of the drawers I come across Rex's file and inside is a copy of the check for a measly few grand that hog-riding, schizo thief gave my father for the San Joaquin Valley groves that were worth close to a million—tangible evidence my father was telling the truth. Even if the groves were mortgaged to the hilt his cut should've been six figures. The date on the check is around the time my father had his law license suspended. He must've been desperate enough to cash it, maybe to pay his own lawyer. Disgusted, I toss the check and the rest of Rex's files in the gap between the fridge and the big, hand carved dining room chairs. Later, when the business of dealing with my father's things is over I will call that man out for being low enough to steal from my father whom he knew was already down and out.

From the heap of papers I make outside of the unit, Lucia tosses them into the flatbed of the pick-up. This process continues for hours until I see Jim's son shoving one of those oversized wooden dining room chairs into the back of the U-Haul. After a couple trips to Goodwill, there is now space to move around inside the unit and I'm able to get out in no time.

"Where are you taking the chairs?" I call out to Jim who has one in his arms. "They're coming home with us."

"But Baby . . ."

The chair is even wider than Jim's muscular shoulders and he needs both hands to carry it. His face is partly obscured by the back of it as if he's behind wooden bars.

My demands are wearing him out quicker than all this moving and he sets down the chair, collapsing in it.

He has no idea how important these chairs and table are to me. He doesn't know that my family used the chairs to protect ourselves against an escaped murderer on the loose. He doesn't know the story about the one night when we returned from a local horse show and encountered two burglars robbing our house, using the table to carry out the goods. One was a white guy with a bandana and the other looked Mexican with a tie-dyed t-shirt. Each had one end of the dining room table that was loaded down with stacks of thinly crafted china from my mother's hutch. The Mexican was backing out first through the front doors.

"What are you doing?" my father asked, just standing there.

"It's okay," the white guy said. "My friend, he lives here."

I will always remember the way my father cocked his head to the side like a dog hearing a high frequency.

"The hell he does. I'm gonna kick your ass, you *boutso gliftie*."

It happened just that fast. My father dropped the keys and lunged right for the white one, clipping the guy at the side of the head with his fist. The table thudded to the sidewalk, my mother's prized gravy boat with the blurry pink flowers being the only casualty, tipping off the table and breaking into pieces on the concrete. My father chased both of the burglars down the street only to lose them in the bushes at the

Norbenger's residence where they also run a dirt and fertilizer company, on the corner.

Running so hard tore the muscles in his belly and required surgery, steel webbing to mesh his flesh back together.

This is a good memory of my father, one of many I want to keep, when he wasn't as strong as he was in the linebacker years of his youth. Still, he was as fearless before the loss of my mother, my brother, and sister as well as his license had aged him and weakened his will to fight.

I sit on Jim's lap. The weight of both of us makes a strange stretching sound coming from the woven seat. I get up quickly.

"I'll nail down some plywood," he says, giving in. "We can't have any of our guests falling through the seats during dinner."

Paper swirls like a tiny tornado in the flatbed as Lucia drives us to the recycling center on Mission Boulevard, past the closed down drive-in theater with a parking lot teeming with tumble weeds and Robin Hood's Sex Shop, a green and white building that's the size of a shoe box with a red bow and arrow painted across the door.

The attendant working the booth at the recycling center has Lucia park on the scale and he weighs us, taking down the number. When we are finished dumping, then we'll drive back on the scale and he'll record what pittance of change we've earned. We have our choice of three different mountains of paper in which to unload.

Lucia backs it up and I jump into the flatbed, and I crouch down and begin. I shove and push and sometimes even kick out the manila folders, depositions bound with brackets and other court transcripts that are the size and heft of fat textbooks. Lucia helps but I do most of the work because I'm faster and because as my father's daughter disposing of what's left of his legal career is my job. Load after load, my hands chafe, nicked with deep paper cuts that sting but never bleed. Sometimes the papers come apart from the folders. Other times the papers fly back at me with the breeze.

I lose count how many trips to the center Lucia and I make. At some point after having dumped a load, I scoot back in the flatbed and rap at the glass with my knuckles. It no longer makes sense to spend what energy I have left crawling out and getting in the front seat.

"Go ahead," I say. "I'll stay back here."

When we're finally all through, the attendant tallies our trips. Ninety-two dollars. The guy who isn't much older than us lets out a shocking whistle.

"That's some paper trail, ladies."

Neither one of us laughs. Not that it isn't funny. We're simply bone tired. Even my rib cage aches from breathing.

In an act of good will I'll send my mother that painting I spared at the last minute. Crying over the phone, she'll insist I stay on the line while she unwraps it.

Lake Tahoe, with a shoreline twelve miles wide and a span of twenty-two miles, provides enough room for her and me to get along, long enough for her to watch me marry. As I've secretly hoped it provides far more—at a recently built casino on the North Shore, seated side by side at the quarter slots, my mother and I share a bucket of coins, trying our luck in a new place. Tahoe is my desired spot to be married because it's where my parents honeymooned, where I imagine they were the most in love. Pitching a tent and laying out sleeping bags at a camp site on the South Side of the lake, they poured red wine into Styrofoam cups. They toasted to their future, their big plans of building my father's law practice from scratch, one client at a time. But then came my sister and then a couple years later me, and the standard fees of divorces and petty criminals weren't enough to keep up with what my parents wanted for us, for our new baby brother and for themselves.

My marriage is weeks away and I've learned from my father not to act like an *ilithios* and worry about what's coming, only what's here in front of me right now. And right now there is nothing before me but a cold and empty concrete space. The material details of the past have been taken away. The files—the private histories, that old refrigerator where my father once kept his ouzo, where I once lost a fake fingernail in the ice tray. It will mean nothing to its next owner and maybe that's a good thing. To let go so as to move on.

No matter how my father may have died or who I suspect, who I know, played a part in it, he is gone. But there is no real proof, there are no real answers and for me, I am a work-in-progress when it comes to accepting what I may never fully understand. In my determination to start I focus on the task at hand. I sweep every corner of the entire unit clean of all the dirt that's collected over the years.

With the cash from my father's old case files I cover the gas for the Ranger. In honor of my father whose name I vow to carry even through marriage, I will meet up with my fiancé and my soon-to-be stepson and blow the rest on salty gyros and some flaming feta at Yanni's.

EPILOGUE

I come alone on that hazy white afternoon, carting a bouquet of white roses that have been spray painted a sunny yellow, thanks to the florist at the shop on the corner who insists nobody will ever be able to tell the difference. They do look freshly cut, center table ready. My father would appreciate the deception. His marker is white with black lettering—Beloved Father, Grandfather, Son, Brother. A decorative black rose winds its way up the side. I imagine if any of his spurned clients, the ones whose fortunes he helped create as well as squander, came by they'd want to add—Shyster and Thief.

The last time I've been to his grave site was when I gave the eulogy and talked in specifics about my father's love for me and my siblings. Toward the end I found a way to slip in his neverending affection for my mother because it was not right that she was singled out from collectively mourning for him too. Before I spoke Uncle Dimitri approached me. "I know you don't want to hear this but Gil wants to say a few words too." Uncle Dimitri shrugged, his eyes squinted up in Yia Yia's way. "What the hell can I do, Paula? They're brothers. I told him he could, but you will get the last word."

Apparently Uncle Dimitri had temporarily forgotten that day how in many ways he helped rear me too. Because I was somewhat surprised he didn't catch on after I reassured him that I was fine with Gil speaking, even offering to go first, that I had no plans providing a pedophile with a captive audience. In an orchestrated protest, Lucia, my sister and brother, followed by my fiancé, headed for the car just as Psycho Gil positioned himself before my father's coffin.

The memory, while still conjuring up old anger, no longer holds as much power. Time may have played a part, but it's my stepson Kyle who ultimately brought me out of my selfish and all consuming grief. He was only in the first grade when Holly died. Everybody had been at the hospital saying their last goodbyes. It was where Kyle and I were headed when I got the call from Jim, telling me to turn around. He didn't want Kyle to remember his mother that way. It was left up to me to forever break a seven-year-old boy's heart by telling him his mommy wouldn't be coming home. "She's gone to another home," I told him, talking as reassuringly as I could over my own sobs, "one with a better view so she can watch out for you. My father and grandfather live up there, too." As he listened Kyle's tears were dollops in his eyes, trapped, with no chance of ever coming down his cheeks. I watched helplessly as my little stepson turned more reserved than most grownups. "I'm too young for this," he'd said to me, throwing his head back against the car seat. Afterward I drove with him to his mother's house and brought some of his clothes along with his aquarium and his pet goldfish, Barracuda, back to the home Jim and I recently bought in Lake Arrowhead. Together Kyle and I stayed busy all afternoon cleaning out the tank, first netting the fish in a salad bowl filled from the tap, then together we dumped out the murky tank water, and with two sponges and real elbow grease we scrubbed clear the algae off the sides. We became closer that day, not because of what I said, but because of how we got through it. Kyle and I let our relationship grow naturally over morning cereal, car rides to and from school and afternoons walking our dogs Maggie and Leo to the park where we've trained Leo since he was a puppy to scramble paws first down the kiddie slide.

Across the lawn a woman stands in front of a fresh mound of earth framed with fly wheels, balloons, and color 8 x 10" photographs of a smiling teenage girl. I am one of many who have suffered loss in a cruel and unexplainable way. As a professor I regularly hear about the sudden tragedies in the families of my students. One student's mother died in a car crash while he was on his honeymoon. Another young female student's boyfriend was murdered, one bullet in the back of his skull, in the alley behind the apartment the two of them shared. The answers why these unthinkable acts happen are only allotted to a lucky few. The rest of us learn to live with only fragments of the truth, as much for the sake of the dead as for ourselves.

Sitting before my father's marker, I search the grass until I find the metal holder hidden beneath and place the roses inside. Then I run my hand across the lettering on his marker. The words, they feel like a stark line of brail, identifying my father to the strangers who pass by on their way to grieve for others. Sadly the words don't say near enough. My father, in his prime, was an enviably good defense lawyer. He could out argue anybody. He taught me how to hold a position and never waiver. He taught me how to stand strong. Later, when he was spent from a profession that forced him to constantly work around the truth, he himself became a cheat as well as having been stolen from himself. But he was also the funniest person I've ever known, cursing everyone and everything out in Greek, from a disgruntled driver who cut him off to the smoking engine of his diesel Mercedes that he failed to fill with oil. At times he rescued me with his frank words of wisdom and sometimes he wrongfully let me down too. But he loved me. He loved me so much he never knew how to say it. Maybe it was the distance between him and my sister and brother that forced him to find the proper words for them.

On some days like this one I am convinced he took his own life. I am convinced he drove away from Sugar Brown's house that night stricken by her dangerous act of disloyalty. It must've hit him that he was just another old fool who had allowed himself to be tricked by a much younger woman. No woman would ever truly love him. My mother had already proven that by walking out on him. By the time he called me from the Kat Nip he had already made up his mind. That was why he had sounded so cryptic, why he had me make that promise. The pills would be easy to find. He could've finished off his own blood pressure prescription or rummaged through Yia Yia's medicine cabinet and taken all of hers. My great grandfather died of suicide, which like other dark secrets in the Priamos family, got buried. I didn't learn of it until well after I'd begun writing this story.

Streaks of sunlight finally break through the gloom and the leaves on the surrounding evergreen trees shimmer and flutter in a slight breeze. Further down from this quiet I can hear the steady flow of freeway traffic, louder now than it was earlier. The woman mourning across the way has already gone. My cell phone rings, and I realize before I even answer that it's getting late. Kyle is wrestling tonight in a tournament up in the mountains and I want to be there. The daughter who stood by her father without hesitation has a family of her own now. Hurriedly, I rise from my father's grave and find my way back home to them.

About Paula Priamos

Paula Priamos teaches at California State University and lives in Southern California with her husband and stepsons. This is her first book.

Books from Etruscan Press

Zarathustra Must Die | Dorian Alexander
The Disappearance of Seth | Kazim Ali
Drift Ice | Jennifer Atkinson
Crow Man | Tom Bailey
Coronology | Claire Bateman
Cinder | Bruce Bond
Peal | Bruce Bond
Toucans in the Arctic | Scott Coffel
Body of a Dancer | Renée E. D'Aoust
Nahoonkara | Peter Grandbois
The Confessions of Doc Williams & Other Poems | William Heyen
A Poetics of Hiroshima | William Heyen
Shoah Train | William Heyen
September 11, 2001, American Writers Respond | Edited by William Heyen
As Easy As Lying | H. L. Hix
Chromatic | H. L. Hix
First Fire, Then Birds | H. L. Hix
God Bless | H. L. Hix
Incident Light | H. L. Hix
Legible Heavens | H. L. Hix
Lines of Inquiry | H. L. Hix
Shadows of Houses | H. L. Hix
Wild and Whirling Words: A Poetic Conversation | H. L. Hix
Art Into Life | Frederick R. Karl
Free Concert: New and Selected Poems | Milton Kessler
Parallel Lives | Michael Lind
The Burning House | Paul Lisicky
Synergos | Robert Manzano
The Gambler's Nephew | Jack Matthews
Venison | Thorpe Moeckel
So Late, So Soon | Carol Moldaw
The Widening | Carol Moldaw
Saint Joe's Passion | JD Schraffenberger
Lies Will Take You Somewhere | Sheila Schwartz
Fast Animal | Tim Seibles

American Fugue | Alexis Stamatis
The Casanova Chronicles | Myrna Stone
White Horse: A Columbian Journey | Diane Thiel
The Fugitive Self | John Wheatcroft

Etruscan Press Is Proud of Support Received From

Wilkes University

Youngstown State University

The Raymond John Wean Foundation

The Ohio Arts Council

The Stephen & Jeryl Oristaglio Foundation

The Nathalie & James Andrews Foundation

The National Endowment for the Arts

The Ruth H. Beecher Foundation

The Bates-Manzano Fund

The New Mexico Community Foundation

Founded in 2001 with a generous grant from the Oristaglio Foundation, Etruscan Press is a nonprofit cooperative of poets and writers working to produce and promote books that nurture the dialogue among genres, achieve a distinctive voice, and reshape the literary and cultural histories of which we are a part.

etruscan press
www.etruscanpress.org

Etruscan Press books may be ordered from

Consortium Book Sales and Distribution
800.283.3572
www.cbsd.com

Small Press Distribution
800.869.7553
www.spdbooks.org

Etruscan Press is a 501(c)(3) nonprofit organization.
Contributions to Etruscan Press are tax deductible
as allowed under applicable law.
For more information, a prospectus,
or to order one of our titles,
contact us at books@etruscanpress.org.